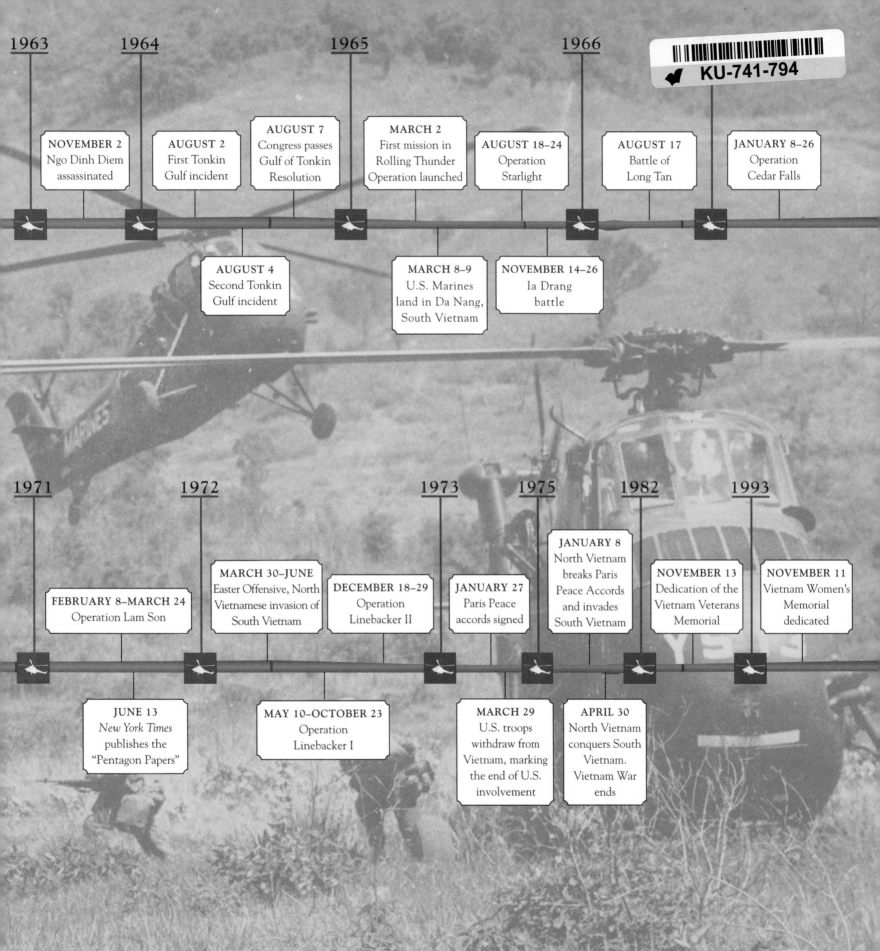

1963

1964

1965

1966

NOVEMBER 2
Ngo Dinh Diem assassinated

AUGUST 2
First Tonkin Gulf incident

AUGUST 7
Congress passes Gulf of Tonkin Resolution

MARCH 2
First mission in Rolling Thunder Operation launched

AUGUST 18–24
Operation Starlight

AUGUST 17
Battle of Long Tan

JANUARY 8–26
Operation Cedar Falls

AUGUST 4
Second Tonkin Gulf incident

MARCH 8–9
U.S. Marines land in Da Nang, South Vietnam

NOVEMBER 14–26
Ia Drang battle

1971

1972

1973

1975

1982

1993

MARCH 30–JUNE
Easter Offensive, North Vietnamese invasion of South Vietnam

DECEMBER 18–29
Operation Linebacker II

JANUARY 27
Paris Peace accords signed

JANUARY 8
North Vietnam breaks Paris Peace Accords and invades South Vietnam

NOVEMBER 13
Dedication of the Vietnam Veterans Memorial

NOVEMBER 11
Vietnam Women's Memorial dedicated

FEBRUARY 8–MARCH 24
Operation Lam Son

JUNE 13
New York Times publishes the "Pentagon Papers"

MAY 10–OCTOBER 23
Operation Linebacker I

MARCH 29
U.S. troops withdraw from Vietnam, marking the end of U.S. involvement

APRIL 30
North Vietnam conquers South Vietnam. Vietnam War ends

10,000 DAYS OF ★ THUNDER

A HISTORY OF THE VIETNAM WAR

PHILIP CAPUTO

10,000 DAYS OF★THUNDER

A HISTORY OF THE VIETNAM WAR

A Byron Preiss Visual Publications, Inc., Book
ATHENEUM BOOKS FOR YOUNG READERS
New York   London   Toronto   Sydney

Dedicated to the families of the 58,209 U.S. servicemen and -women who gave their lives in Vietnam

Atheneum Books for Young Readers
An imprint of Simon & Schuster Children's Publishing Division
1230 Avenue of the Americas
New York, New York 10020

Text copyright © 2005 by Philip Caputo
All other materials copyright © 2005 by Byron Preiss Visual
Publications, Inc.

Front jacket photo caption: A combined U.S. and South Vietnamese
  action against Viet Cong guerrillas in 1962.
Title page photo caption: U.S. soldier protects South Vietnamese
  villagers during a mission to round up suspected Viet Cong.

The text of this book is set in Goudy.
Manufactured in the United States of America
First Edition

10 9 8 7 6 5 4 3 2 1

Library of Congress Cataloging-in-Publication Data
Caputo, Philip.
10,000 days of thunder : a history of the Vietnam War / Philip
Caputo.—1st ed.
p.   cm.
ISBN 0-689-86231-8 (ISBN-13: 978-0-689-86231-1)
1. Vietnamese Conflict, 1961–1975—Juvenile literature.
2. Vietnamese conflict, 1961–1975—United States—Juvenile
literature. I. Title.
DS557.7C36 2005
959.704'3—dc22   2004015468

PHOTO CREDITS:
Air Force Archives: p. 107
AP/Wide World Photos: pp. 7, 9, 11, 34, 37, 39, 42, 44, 46, 47,
  52, 62 *(left)*, 63, 68, 69, 71, 73, 79, 81, 89, 91, 93, 97, 98, 100,
  101, 102, 104, 105, 106, 110, 111, 112,113, 115, 116, and 119
© Bettmann/CORBIS: pp. 13, 17, 43, 53, 57, 65, 83, and 85
© Hulton-Deutsch/CORBIS: pp. 12 and 15
John F. Kennedy Library: pp. 22 and 23
Library of Congress: pp. 48, 78
Lyndon Baines Johnson Library: pp. 29, 70, 87, and 99
Modern Military Records, National Archives: p. 18
National Archives: pp. 16, 19, 24, 25, 26, 27, 30, 31, 32, 33, 36,
  40, 41, 45, 49, 51, 55, 58, 59, 60, 61, 62 *(right)*, 64, 67, 72, 75,
  76, 77, 80, 82, 86, 90, 94, 95, and 108
National League of Families of American Prisoners and Missing
  in Southeast Asia: p. 114
Naval Institute Archives: pp. 54 and 117
Nixon Presidential Materials Staff, National Archives: pp. 79, 96,
  and 109
Philip Caputo: p. 10
William Robert Hodder: p. 88

TABLE OF CONTENTS

The Vietnam War has three dubious distinctions: It was the longest and the most unpopular war in American history and the only war America ever lost.

Whether as advisors to the South Vietnamese Army or as combat troops directly engaged in fighting the Viet Cong and the North Vietnamese Army, U.S. soldiers served in Vietnam from 1959 to 1975, making the war twice as long as the War of Independence (1775–1783).

In some ways, the war was easier on troops than previous conflicts had been for their fathers and grandfathers. U.S. fighting men were not "in for the duration" of the war as they had been in World War I and World War II but served fixed tours of duty of one year (except for marines who served for thirteen months). Sophisticated medical techniques and helicopter evacuations from the battlefield greatly reduced a soldier's chances of dying from his wounds. America's overwhelming superiority in firepower also kept casualties down. If they got into trouble, soldiers could count on devastating air strikes and artillery barrages to help them get out of it.

In other ways, the war was much more difficult. Although there were many instances of conventional-style fighting, the war was mostly an unconventional, guerilla conflict fought against an elusive enemy in thick jungles, where it was difficult to see much farther than a few yards in any direction. While certain areas of Vietnam were safer than others, there were no established front lines; the enemy could be behind you as well as in front of you.

The Viet Cong, as Communist guerillas were called, were not as well-armed or well-trained as their North Vietnamese Army allies, but they were masters of bushcraft and hit-and-run tactics, skilled in staging ambushes and in land-mine warfare. They were active mostly at night, appearing and disappearing like ghosts. One of their favorite tactics was to set an ambush by placing an electronically controlled mine or booby trap on a trail used by American patrols, then the Viet Cong ambushers would hide nearby and detonate the mine by remote, when the patrol arrived, shoot a brief burst of automatic rifle fire at the same time, and then vanish into the jungle.

I was a lieutenant in Vietnam. My platoon (a platoon is a unit consisting of about thirty to forty men) was caught in just such an ambush one day in 1965. In seconds, nine of my men were wounded, five of them gravely, and we never saw the enemy, never had a chance to shoot back. I served in Vietnam with two different marine infantry battalions in 1965 and 1966. One of those battalions suffered well over four hundred dead and wounded in its first four months in combat. My company was whittled down from 175 to 90 men during that period, and today I can find the names of 16 of my close friends carved on the Vietnam War Memorial—"the Wall"—in Washington, D.C.

To make matters even more difficult, the Viet Cong seldom wore uniforms. They were indistinguishable from civilians. A rice-paddy farmer plowing his field behind a water buffalo was as likely to be a guerilla fighter as not. It was often impossible for an American soldier to tell who was the enemy and who wasn't until he was shot at—and then it would be too late.

The climate and terrain made for tough conditions to fight in. Vietnam is a tropical country consisting of rugged, mountainous jungle; vast marshes; and rice paddies that turn into swamps during the monsoon

Opposite: U.S. Marines wade ashore at Da Nang, South Vietnam, on March 18, 1965.

season, when rains fall nearly every day for six months. During the other six months—the dry season—temperatures of 100 degrees Fahrenheit are common. The extreme heat could inflict more casualties than the enemy. I recall one patrol when a dozen marines in our company were taken out of action due to heatstroke and heat exhaustion. The temperature that day was an astounding 117 degrees!

One other thing made Vietnam tough on U.S. soldiers—their youth. In the three previous major wars of the twentieth century—World Wars I, II, and the Korean War—the average age of the fighting man was twenty-six. In Vietnam it was only nineteen—an army of boys. Men of a more mature age are better able to cope with the stresses and horrors of combat than teenagers who aren't even old enough to legally drink or to vote. (In the 1960s, the voting age, which is now eighteen, was twenty-one.) As a result thousands of Vietnam veterans were emotionally and psychologically scarred by their experiences, many for life.

Recovering from those hidden wounds wasn't made any easier by the reception they were given once they came home. In contrast to the ceremonial welcomes that greeted veterans of previous wars, soldiers returning from Vietnam were treated with indifference, contempt, and sometimes outright hostility. Americans had become so disillusioned with the war that they often blamed the fighting men for the moral and military failures of their leaders. When I was home on leave, some antiwar activists threw a bagful of food scraps in my face because my "high and tight" military haircut marked me as a soldier.

People often ask me why the United States lost the war. To this day Americans have a hard time accepting the fact that the most powerful nation on Earth, with its mighty economy and large military resources, could not prevail against a small, mainly agricultural nation composed mostly of peasants. Many reasons have been given, some valid and some questionable, but in my mind America's defeat is best explained by the nature of the war.

It was a civil war, and therefore it was as much a political as it was a military contest. As you will read in the following pages, Vietnam had a history of armed resistance against foreign conquerors going back two thousand years. For the last half of the nineteenth century and the first half of the twentieth, it was a colony in the French Empire. The Vietnamese overthrew the French in 1954 after a long, bloody conflict, and were looking forward to becoming a united, independent nation when the politics of the Cold War intervened and foreign powers, including the United States, divided the country into North and South Vietnam.

In the eyes of the North Vietnamese and the Viet Cong, their battle against the Americans was a continuation of the struggle for unity and independence from outside influences. For that reason they had the active or tacit support of the civilian population—not all of them but enough to make it very difficult for the United States to prevail in the war. The American army in Vietnam was, in effect, fighting not another army but almost an entire *nation*. It was a limited war for the United States, but an all-out war of total commitment for the North Vietnamese and Viet Cong. Their leaders knew that if they could hang on long enough, the United States would eventually tire of the struggle. In fact that is what happened. There is an old saying in military circles stating that the guerilla fighter doesn't have to win to win; he wins by not losing.

General Vo Nguyen Giap, the North Vietnamese

Opposite: U.S. Marine helicopters drop troops into a suspected Viet Cong area.

Above: The author in Vietnam.

In 1990, along with several other American warriors turned novelists and poets, I was invited to a dinner by the Da Nang chapter of the Vietnamese Writers Union. A poet named Ngan Vinh gave a brief speech and then read one of his works, "After the Rain in the Forest." He was a striking-looking man, tall for a Vietnamese at five feet nine inches tall, with a lean, muscular build and a shock of thick, black hair graying at the temples. During the war, Vinh had been a platoon leader like me, commanding forty-two men in the First Battalion, 40th Brigade, of the North Vietnamese Army, and his poem was about carrying a wounded comrade to safety after a battle in the monsoon of 1967. The words and imagery—the weight of the man on his shoulders, blood mixed with rain spilling into the mud of the trail—astonished me because they were so like the words and images of a poem I had written in 1966. It was called "Infantry in the Monsoon," and it was about carrying wounded comrades in the rain.

I mentioned this coincidence to Vinh after the meal. He asked me to read the poem, but I didn't have it with me, nor could I remember more than a few lines, which I recited at his request. We got to talking and discovered that his battalion and mine had operated in the same valley southwest of Da Nang in early 1966. Though we determined that we had never fought each other, that was close enough. Vinh filled two glasses with vodka and said we had to drink together. We tossed our glasses back, and then Vinh embraced me and said, "You and me, Philip, we are brothers in arms," and that night, June 21, 1990, was when the Vietnam War ended for me.

defense minister and overall commander in chief of the Communist forces, gave me an insight into this strategy when I met him in Hanoi in 1990. I'd mentioned to the diminutive and aging Giap (he was, by then, in his late seventies and stood only five feet three inches tall), that I could think of only a few instances when U.S. forces actually lost a battle in Vietnam in the classic sense. Nine times out of ten, they'd won.

"Yes, they did," he replied, "but in the end it didn't make any difference."

In other words, the United States had won the battles but lost the war.

The war began for me on March 8, 1965, when my battalion landed at the port city of Da Nang. I was rotated home on July 12, 1966, but that is not when the war ended for me, because wars have a way of going on and on in your mind and your soul long after you've left the battlefield.

Opposite: After receiving sniper fire, U.S. Marines set fire to the village of Cam Ne.

QUICK FACTS

● One of the ironies of Communism was that Marx intended it to unite workers of the industrialized nations. Russia in the 1800s was a largely agricultural nation that was so politically backward it still practiced feudalism, a system not seen in Western Europe since the Middle Ages. Marx never imagined that Russia would be the place his political philosophy would take hold.

● The Soviet Union was composed of the countries Armenia, Azerbaijan, Belorussia, Estonia, Georgia, Kazakhstan, Kirghizia, Latvia, Lithuania, Moldavia, Russia, Tadzhikistan, Turkmenistan, Ukraine, and Uzbekistan.

Above: Leon Trotsky, as People's Commissar for Military and Naval Affairs in the USSR during the early years of the republic, was responsible for creating and training the Red Army.

Two opposing political philosophies dominated international relations in the twentieth century. They were democracy and Communism, and the extreme nature of their differences made it inevitable that they would be in conflict, both militarily and diplomatically, until one side was defeated. The leading, and most powerful, democratic nation was the United States. The most powerful Communist nation was the Union of Soviet Socialist Republics, commonly called the USSR, the Soviet Union, or Russia, after the largest nation within the Soviet Union.

Democracy, created by the Greeks around 500 B.C., is a system of government composed of individuals elected to office by the voting population. These elected officials (in the United States these include governors, senators, members of Congress, and the president and vice president) create laws and government policy. Regular elections are held so that the people have an opportunity to choose, if they so desire, new people to lead and govern them.

Communism was created in 1848, when the educator turned philosopher Karl Marx, the father of Communism, and his disciple, Friedrich Engels, published *The Communist Manifesto*, a forty-page pamphlet that was a scathing response to the social injustices inflicted on the European working class by industrialists. In the *Manifesto*, Marx and Engels called on the working class to revolt against their oppressors.

Later in 1867, in his book *Das Kapital*, Marx expanded on the Communist theme in detail, and this book became the bible for Communist leaders around the world. Marx's goal was to end the social injustices and inequities he saw existing between the very rich and the very poor. Once the Communists had seized control of the government, they would transform their nation into a worker's paradise, in which the rich would have their wealth confiscated and redistributed to the working class; private property would be abolished; everyone would receive "cradle-to-grave" healthcare and social services; and colonialism would end. Also, Communists promised that no one would ever be without a job. Communists claimed that one hundred percent employment was possible under their rule because the government, not private individuals, controlled the economy.

Even though many industrial workers throughout the world labored twelve or more hours a day, six to seven days a week for low pay, Communism was

Opposite: Karl Marx, the founder of Communism.

slow to establish itself. One reason for this was that governments in most of the industrialized nations were already instituting some of the reforms that Communists wanted, such as shorter working hours and higher pay standards. Though Communist parties formed in a variety of countries, Marx, who had lived in poverty all of his adult life, died at age sixty-four in 1883 without seeing one Communist takeover of any nation.

Marx's most successful follower was a Russian, Vladimir Ilyich Ulyanov, who began promoting for a Communist revolution of Russia in 1893. Because of this, the Russian government's secret police marked him for death, forcing him into exile and into changing his name to the alias, Lenin. In 1903, at a London conference of Russian Communist exiles, a schism split the group into two parts: Bolshevik (Russian for "majority") and Menshevik (Russian for "minority"). Lenin emerged as the leader of the Bolshevik Party, and Julius Martov was made the leader of the Mensheviks. After several years of revolutionary activities in Russia, on October 25, 1917 the Bolsheviks, led by Lenin and Leon Trotsky, seized legislative power and installed a Communist government. Lenin then began to ruthlessly establish control over the country. He ordered political rivals, such as the Mensheviks and anyone who held power in the previous government, imprisoned or killed. Thousands of people died. In 1919 the Communist International (Comintern) was organized to coordinate Communist activities throughout the world in order to overthrow capitalist governments.

In that year, a Communist party was formed in the United States, which many perceived as a threat to democracy. This formation sparked the first anti-Communist reaction within the country, forcing the Communist Party to go underground. In December 1922 the USSR was officially formed. Lenin died about a year later, on January 21, 1924, and a power struggle between the top Communist leaders began. Joseph Stalin eventually emerged victorious, and Leon Trotsky was forced into exile. Stalin acted swiftly to concentrate all power under him, and within a few years became a dictator. Under his rule Communism in the Soviet Union became even more brutal and tyrannical than it had ever been. The most famous examples of his tyranny

Opposite: Trotsky enlisted males—both young and old—into the ranks of the Red Army. Here a group of boys has lined up to await inspection by Trotsky.

were the series of purges in the 1930s, in which Stalin had executed almost all of the top and senior officers in the army and many rival political leaders.

Communist parties in the western democracies were never able to control any government. Only a Communist revolution in the early 1930s in China, led by Mao Tse-tung, against the weak Nationalist government headed by Jiang Jie-shi, gained any headway, ultimately seizing control in 1949.

The hostility between the Communist Soviet Union and the United States, Great Britain, France, and other democracies was set aside in 1941 in order to battle a greater, mutual enemy—the Axis nations of Nazi Germany, Italy, and Japan during World War II. In 1945, following the defeat of the Axis, the old suspicions resurfaced.

World War II had devastated the Soviet Union. Nazi Germany had invaded the country, killing tens of millions of people—civilians and soldiers—and destroying countless cities and industries. Anxious to prevent another such war and fearful of the atomic bomb, which at that time only the United States possessed, Stalin installed friendly Communist governments in Eastern Europe, creating a "buffer zone" between Western Europe and the Soviet Union. Stalin's actions alarmed the western nations. Even though the United States had the atomic bomb, it did not want to use it to stop Communist aggression because doing so might start a third world war. In 1949 the United States helped establish the North Atlantic Treaty Organization (NATO), a military alliance of Western European nations designed to protect against Soviet attack. It also stopped a Soviet-sponsored Communist attempt to seize control of Greece. In 1949 the USSR successfully exploded its first atomic bomb. Together with Communist China, it gave aid to Communist North Korea when it attacked democratic South Korea in the Korean War (1950–1953). In response to NATO, the Soviet Union formed a military alliance with the Communist Eastern European nations in 1955 called the Warsaw Treaty Organization.

Although both the United States and the Soviet Union had nuclear capabilities, this threat did not lead either of them to peacefully settle their differences. Instead it caused them to fight on non-nuclear battlefields in regional conflicts, a series of struggles that came to be called the Cold War. The Korean War was one such conflict. The largest of them was to become the Vietnam War.

Above: St. Paul's Church seen during the bombing of London in World War II.

Opposite: Important political events and parades in the Soviet Union were always held in Moscow's Red Square. Here, a crowd listens to Leon Trotsky give a speech.

ORIGINS OF THE VIETNAM WAR
PART ONE: FRENCH COLONIALISM IN VIETNAM

QUICK FACTS

- Ho Chi Minh (Vietnamese for "He Who Enlightens") was the most famous alias for Nguyen Tat Thanh, who used more than one hundred aliases. His second most famous alias was Nguyen Ai Quoc (Nguyen the Patriot). He used the aliases to avoid capture, imprisonment, and assassination by governments and troops who hated what he represented.

- Ho Chi Minh did not live to see Vietnam united. He died on September 2, 1969, at the age of seventy-nine, six years before North Vietnam conquered South Vietnam.

- "Viet Minh" is a shortened version of "Viet Nam Doc Lap Dong Minh" (League for the Independence of Vietnam). Originally it included both non-Communist and Communist patriots. It began converting to an all-Communist organization after 1951.

- During the 1954 Viet Minh siege of the French outpost at Dien Bien Phu, U.S. president Dwight Eisenhower and his top advisors seriously considered sending troops and using tactical nuclear bombs to help the French against the Viet Minh.

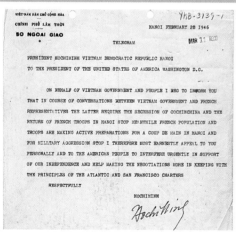

Above: A telegram from Ho Chi Minh to President Truman, appealing for his support of Vietnamese independence from France.

While there is no official start date for the Vietnam War, it is generally considered to have begun on March 8–9, 1965, when, under the orders of President Johnson, the first combat troops landed in South Vietnam. The war for the United States ended on March 29, 1973, when the last U.S. troops were withdrawn. However, America's involvement in Vietnam began much earlier, when it first sent aid to the French colonial rulers in 1950 and did not entirely end until the South Vietnamese government surrendered to the North Vietnamese Army on April 30, 1975.

The story of the Vietnam War is also the story of the man who would become modern Vietnam's foremost patriot, Ho Chi Minh. Ho's first attempt to secure Vietnam's independence from France occurred in 1919, when he was in Paris during the drafting of the Treaty of Versailles, which would end World War I. Ho fearlessly, and in vain, petitioned the victorious Allies to agree to an end to French colonialism in Southeast Asia. During this time, Ho embraced the political philosophy called Communism, which called for the end to all colonialism.

At the beginning of World War II, in 1940–1942, the Japanese Army invaded and conquered the lightly defended Indochina peninsula of Thailand, Laos, Vietnam, Cambodia, Myanmar, and Malay Peninsula. Shortly after the invasion, Ho and his Communist followers returned to Vietnam to organize guerilla operations to fight the Japanese. They created the Viet Minh, a nationalist organization composed of Communist and non-Communist Vietnamese patriots who actively worked for independence. Believing the Allied forces of America and England fighting the Japanese in Indochina would help them achieve their goal, the Viet Minh provided them with intelligence assistance.

After the Japanese defeat in 1945, Ho, the leader of the Viet Minh, declared Vietnamese independence on September 2, 1945. Ho also petitioned President Harry S Truman for help. But the American government refused because it thought France's colonial rule could better guarantee the region's stability. In response, the Viet Minh launched a guerilla war against the French Army in Vietnam, culminating with the French Army's defeat on May 7, 1954, with the fifty-six-day siege of Dien Bien Phu, a French military outpost in North Vietnam. This battle signaled the end of French colonial rule in the region. It did not mean that the war in Vietnam was over.

Opposite: A French Foreign Legionnaire patrol in the Red River Delta region of Vietnam.

QUICK FACTS

- The 1954 Geneva Conference established a temporary border between North and South Vietnam at the Ben Hai River on the 17th parallel, at approximately the middle of the country. This border became a 5-mile-wide buffer zone called the Demilitarized Zone, or DMZ, because the treaty prohibited ground or artillery activity in this area. The North Vietnamese government did not observe this restriction.

- Ho Chi Minh predicted that the Indochinese war against France would be the war of the tiger (Vietnamese) and the elephant (foreigners). Because the tiger could not fight the elephant as an equal, it would ambush it, slash the elephant with its claws, hide in the jungle, then attack again. Eventually the elephant would bleed to death. This philosophy worked against both France and the United States.

- In 1954, following the French departure from Vietnam, President Eisenhower asked the army's chief of staff, General Matthew Ridgeway, to conduct a study of what American military aid would be needed to help the South Vietnamese defeat the Communists in Vietnam. Ridgeway reported that the United States would have to commit between 500,000 and 1 million men. President Eisenhower decided this was an impossible option, so instead chose to send minimal aid in the form of weapons, supplies, economic aid, and military and political advisors.

While the siege at Dien Bien Phu was raging, a conference was held in 1954 in Geneva, Switzerland, to draft a treaty for an orderly transfer of power from the French to the Viet Minh. When the Viet Minh won the siege, they hoped it would mean Vietnam would be free of French rule and influence. Even though the French were ready to leave Vietnam, they continued to fight the Viet Minh in order to extract economic concessions that would produce a treaty favorable to France.

Unfortunately the Geneva Conference was held during the Cold War, a period of severe tension between the United States, the Soviet Union, and the People's Republic of China (Communist China). Though the Viet Minh had won the battle at Dien Bien Phu, the United States intervened and refused to allow Communists to take over all of Vietnam. Because the Soviet Union and Communist China, who had sent military and economic aid to the Viet Minh, did not want to risk a war with the United States by backing the Viet Minh too strongly, on July 20, 1954, Ho and his followers had to accept revised terms of the treaty: Communist Viet Minh would govern the northern half of the country (the Democratic Republic of Vietnam, or North Vietnam), and a democratic group supported by the United States would administer the southern half (the Republic of Vietnam, or South Vietnam).

This temporary division was scheduled to end two years later, in 1956, with a general election designed to unite the whole country. Under the terms of the treaty, the United States was allowed to intervene in creating a new government for Vietnam, so it became very active in the politics of the country. The United States recognized that Communists were better organized than the other political parties and would win the election. Therefore the United States delayed the event in order to allow the non-Communist political parties time to become strong enough to ensure a fair election. Because the country did not have a strong democratic tradition, it was difficult to build a strong political party to oppose the Viet Minh. The United States had continually postponed the election until finally the Viet Minh realized that the only way to unite Vietnam would be to conquer South Vietnam.

The compromise that effectively divided Vietnam into two countries did not satisfy either side. The Geneva Conference ensured that it would only be a matter of time before fighting would resume in Vietnam.

CHINA

BURMA

NORTH VIETNAM

Hanoi ⊛
● Haiphong

Gulf of Tonkin

LAOS

● Chu Lai

THAILAND

DMZ

● Hue

● Da Nang

I CORPS

● Chu Lai

South China Sea

II CORPS

● Qui Nhon

CAMBODIA

SOUTH VIETNAM

● Ban Me Thuot

Gulf of Thailand

● Loc Ninh

III CORPS

Cu Chi ● Bien Hoa ● Xuan Loc

⊛

IV CORPS

● Saigon

Mekong Delta

★ Vietnam ★

Ca Mau Peninsula

N
W E
S

0   50   100 miles

0   50   100 kilometers

ORIGINS OF THE VIETNAM WAR
PART THREE: THE REASON FOR AMERICAN INTERVENTION

QUICK FACTS

- Ngo Dinh Diem became the first president of democratic South Vietnam in 1955. His government was unstable and lacked popular support. In 1963 he was assassinated. A power struggle between the top military leaders in South Vietnam occurred over the next 2 years, during which 9 governments came and went. Finally in 1967 general elections were held and General Nguyen Van Thieu was elected president and General Nguyen Cao Ky was elected vice president. Their government remained in control of South Vietnam until the end of the war.

- Vietnam is a tropical country that has two seasons. The rainy season, which lasts roughly from May to September, is notable for its monsoons, which could be so strong that they would halt all combat operations for weeks. If soldiers weren't careful, their shoes and clothing would literally rot away. The dry season, which lasts roughly from October to April, is notable for its furnacelike heat, often reaching more than 100 degrees.

Above: President John F. Kennedy in the Oval Office signing a proclamation that established a quarantine, which barred American businesses and people from working with or visiting Cuba.

By 1954 it looked as if Communists might be successful in their oft-stated goal to take over the world. In the years immediately following the end of World War II, Communist governments were installed by Stalin in a number of countries. Germany, defeated in World War II, had been divided by the conquering Allied Powers along the Elbe River in 1945, forming democratic West Germany and Communist East Germany. Meanwhile in Asia, China had fallen to Communism led by Mao Tse-tung. In the Korean War, a three-year conflict that ended in 1953, Communist-ruled North Korea had almost conquered the democratic South Korea. The United States, together with the international peacekeeping organization, the United Nations, came to the rescue of South Korea. Total defeat of North Korea was made impossible when Communist China rushed to the aid of its fellow Communist country. A seesaw battle went on for several months, ending in an uneasy truce in 1953 at the border between South and North Korea.

The U.S. concern about the danger of Communist expansion increased in 1959, when Cuba, a Caribbean island-nation less than one hundred miles south of Florida, fell to Communism, led by Fidel Castro. On October 15, 1962, U.S. intelligence learned that the Soviet Union was building nuclear missile launching sites on the island. These areas would target cities and military stations throughout the United States. The American government could not tolerate such a threat, especially so close to American soil. This incident, called the Cuban Missile Crisis, brought the United States and the Soviet Union to the brink of a nuclear war. It was peacefully concluded with the dismantling of these launch sites and an agreement between the United States and the Soviet Union that Cuba would not be supplied with nuclear weapons.

Against this frightening backdrop, the United States government believed that if the Viet Minh took over all of Vietnam, Communism would infiltrate the neighboring nations of Laos, Cambodia, Thailand, and Indonesia, a belief based on the "domino theory." The U.S. also began to doubt South Vietnam's ability to defend itself against attack from North Vietnam's strong army and from Communist guerillas of the National Liberation Front, known as the Viet Cong, located in South Vietnam.

With Cuba as a clear reminder of Communist threat, the stage was set for America's participation in a war that lasted ten thousand days—the Vietnam War.

Opposite: An aerial photograph of a nuclear warhead bunker under construction in Cuba.

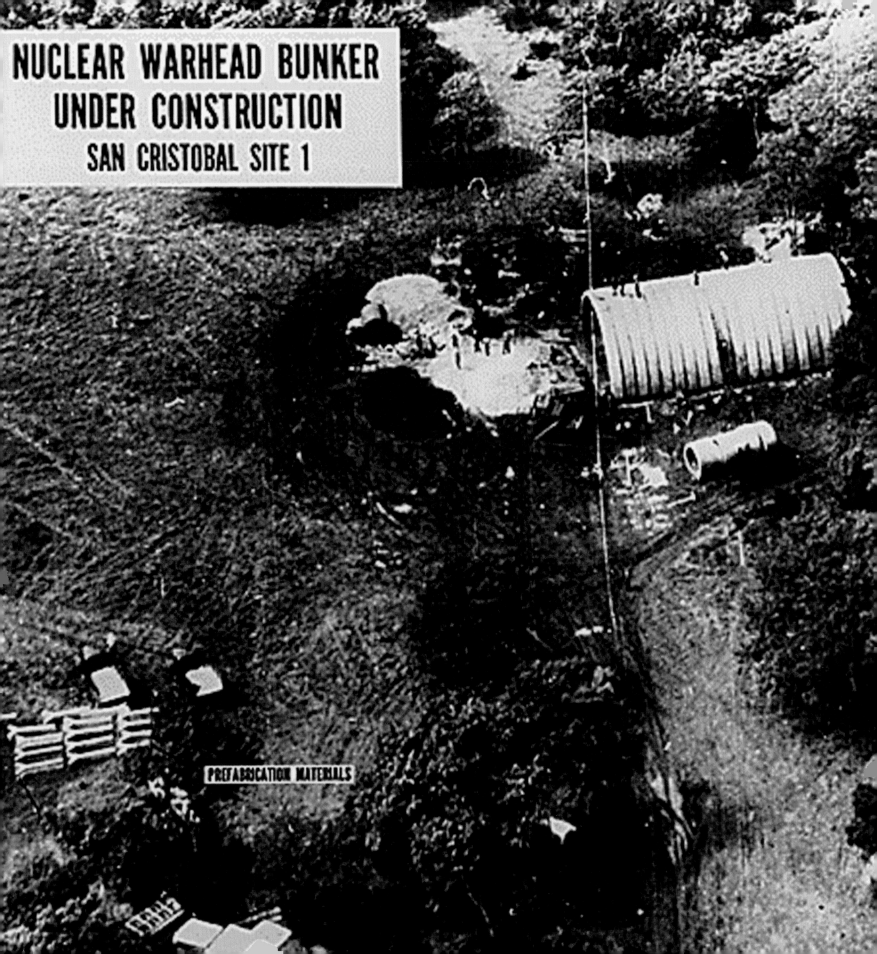

NUCLEAR WARHEAD BUNKER
UNDER CONSTRUCTION
SAN CRISTOBAL SITE 1

PREFABRICATION MATERIALS

QUICK FACTS

- "Viet Cong" is short for "Viet Nam Cong San"—"Vietnamese Communist." The Viet Cong got the slang name "Charlie" from the U.S. military radio nomenclature for the letters V and C—*Victor* and *Charlie.*

- Captured Viet Cong who agreed to work for the South Vietnamese government and serve on the front lines with U.S. troops were called "Kit Carson scouts," after the famous American-Indian fighter of the Southwest.

- The United States forces tried many methods and tools to find the hiding Viet Cong. One was an invention named the "Olfactronic Personnel Detector." The troops called it the "People Sniffer" because it was supposed to "smell" the ammonia and methane gas given off by human urine and excrement. Another personnel detector was the Air-Delivered Seismic Intruder Device (ADSID), which was supposed to broadcast seismic readings caused by the vibrations of moving people or vehicles. Neither were very successful.

Above: A marine walks away from a Viet Cong complex composed of bunkers and tunnels that the marines have just destroyed.

At the conclusion of hostilities between the French and the Viet Minh in 1954 and in accordance with the treaty, all Communists were supposed to move into North Vietnam. Non-Communists in the north regrouped in the south. The Viet Minh organization, which initially contained both Communist and non-Communist patriots united to achieve Vietnam's independence, was dissolved. Now the Vietnamese Communist Party controlled the north, and a democratic government was being organized in the south with the assistance of the United States.

The Communist leaders in North Vietnam disregarded the conditions of the treaty and instructed an estimated five thousand to ten thousand Communist soldiers to remain behind and under cover in South Vietnam and to await further instructions. These soldiers formed the core of the guerilla organization that came to be known as the "Viet Cong." Viet Cong was what Americans and the South Vietnamese called the members of the organization officially known as the National Front for the Liberation of South Vietnam, sometimes known by the shorter name of the National Liberation Front.

Almost immediately, the Viet Cong began to commit acts of terrorism, ranging from the assassination of low-level government and civil officials and their families, to setting booby traps, to collecting taxes in the form of rice and other food from rural villagers, to recruiting men and women into its ranks and conducting hit-and-run raids.

The Viet Cong included people from all walks of life, from illiterate peasants to highly educated professionals. Dr. Vo Hoang Le was a Viet Cong surgeon who performed a number of lifesaving operations in the middle of battles. He recalled one occasion when an American armored unit attacked a base on a plantation called Dat Thiet: "We were operating on a soldier wounded in the stomach when the enemy tanks arrived. We took off our gowns, put the patient in a hammock, grabbed our equipment and ran. We made it to the next village. . . . We halted to continue the operation in [the] hammock. The instruments were filthy . . . so we sterilized them [using] alcohol. We sewed up the punctures in his intestines and stitched up his abdomen with nylon threads taken from enemy parachutes. The wounded soldier survived."

Opposite: A Viet Cong soldier in a tunnel.

Opposite: Soldiers in the South Vietnamese Army training in the jungle.

QUICK FACTS

- U.S. Military Assistance Command Vietnam (MACV) was created in 1962. Its first commander was General Paul D. Harkins. When his tour as commander ended in 1964, he was succeeded by General William Westmoreland who oversaw the integration of MAAG into MACV.

- In English, simple tasks quickly done are said to be as "easy as pie." In Vietnamese, they are "like eating dog's brain." Dogs are considered food in Vietnam the same way pigs and cattle are in the United States.

- Before 1965 the U.S. government encouraged married American advisors to have their families live with them in South Vietnam. One such advisor was U. S. Navy Captain Bill Hardcastle, who had with him his wife and high school–aged daughter, Susan. When Susan went to school, a bus with two guards armed with automatic weapons would pick her up. As she rode to school, she looked out bus windows that were covered with wire mesh screens to keep out Viet Cong grenades.

Above: A twelve-year-old Army of the Republic of Vietnam (ARVN) soldier in front of buildings that were destroyed during a battle.

The independent nation of the Republic of Vietnam (South Vietnam) was created on October 26, 1955. Less than a week later, the U.S. Military Assistance Advisory Group Vietnam (MAAG, Vietnam) was formed. Its mission was to provide advisors and other military assistance, including weapons and equipment, to help train and reorganize the Army of the Republic of Vietnam, or ARVN. If successful, the South Vietnamese Army could defend itself against the Viet Cong and the North Vietnamese Army without the additional aid of U.S. combat forces.

The MAAG advisors encountered both highly competent commanders in South Vietnam and those who were political appointees and invariably incompetent. The advisors worked with all of the commanders, doing their part to help fight the spread of Communism. Over the years, the number of advisors increased from a few hundred in the 1950s to approximately sixteen thousand by the time combat troops arrived in 1965.

As Viet Cong and North Vietnamese Army incursions and attacks increased, U.S. wives and children were ordered to leave South Vietnam because of the increasing danger, and more advisors and military aid were sent in. In 1965 Major Norman Schwarzkopf was one such advisor, assigned to an ARVN airborne unit in 1965. When his unit was given a search-and-destroy mission against the enemy hiding in the jungle, one of the many things Schwarzkopf noted was the kind of food the ARVN troops took and how they transported it. "Each man had live ducks and chickens tied to his belt, with their beaks taped so they couldn't make noise," he wrote. They also had in their rucksacks fresh pork and beef, and cans of sardines. Across their chests they strapped a large brown tube that contained rice.

At one point during Maj. Schwarzkopf's tour, a unit of ARVN engineers completed construction of a bridge and invited him to attend the bridge-blessing ceremony. During the ceremony, each attendee was given a large glass partially filled with Scotch whiskey. The engineers then slaughtered a pig, topped off the glasses with its blood, and made a toast. Schwarzkopf gulped his drink down. His South Vietnamese counterparts were both surprised and pleased by his following of their custom. The previous American advisor had not.

On August 2, 1964, the USS *Maddox*, a destroyer on an intelligence-gathering mission in the Gulf of Tonkin, which was off the coast of North Vietnam and considered international waters, was attacked by three North Vietnamese torpedo boats. Two days later the *Maddox* and another American destroyer, the *Turner Joy*, reported that they were under attack by North Vietnamese torpedo boats. These two events, known as the Tonkin Gulf Incidents, would cause the United States to dramatically escalate its military presence and thus the war in Vietnam.

After the second assault, President Johnson ordered retaliatory strikes against the port where the torpedo boats were harbored. At the same time, he sent a message to Congress that said, in part, "The North Vietnamese regime has constantly sought to take over South Vietnam. . . . It has systematically conducted a campaign of subversion . . . in South Vietnamese territory." He then requested Congress to authorize an increase in military aid to the government of South Vietnam. What he did not do was ask Congress to declare war on North Vietnam. He had many reasons for not doing so, the most important being that he did not want to give the Soviet Union and Communist China a reason to dramatically increase their aid to North Vietnam, thus increasing the risk of starting World War III.

On August 7, 1964, in a joint resolution of Congress, H.J. RES 1145, commonly known as the Gulf of Tonkin Resolution, passed by a vote of eighty-eight to two in the Senate and unanimously in the House of Representatives. It gave President Johnson the power "to take all necessary steps, including the use of armed force" to help South Vietnam. Furthermore the resolution had no expiration date—that was left up to the discretion of the president or by concurrent resolution of the Congress.

During the debate prior to the passing of the resolution, Senator Wayne Morse of Oregon, one of the two dissenting senators and, as was Johnson, a Democrat, stated, "I believe that within the next century, future generations will look with dismay and great disappointment upon a Congress which is now about to make such a historic mistake."

By then it was too late. In 1965, by order of the president, American combat troops were once again marching off to battle. This time in Vietnam.

Opposite: President Lyndon B. Johnson.

QUICK FACTS

- The Viet Cong often conducted ambushes using "spider holes." These were heavily camouflaged foxholes, which usually held one soldier and were virtually invisible. A soldier in a spider hole would usually wait until a patrol had just passed his position before throwing off the camouflage cover and firing on the patrol from the rear.

- The Viet Cong were notorious for setting booby traps. One common booby trap was a camouflaged pit that contained punji stakes. Punji stakes were sharpened bamboo sticks that usually were coated with feces, thus causing infection in a wound.

- Corporal Robert E. O'Malley was one of two marines who earned America's highest military decoration, the Medal of Honor, on the first day of battle. His citation read, in part, "Although three times wounded in this encounter, and facing imminent death from a fanatic and determined enemy, he steadfastly refused evacuation and continued to cover his squad's boarding of the helicopters."

Above: A young marine on a beach shortly after an amphibious landing.

To administer the war, Military Assistance Command Vietnam (MACV) organized South Vietnam into four tactical zones. The northernmost was I Corps operated by the marines, followed by II Corps, III Corps, and IV Corps, all run by the army. In 1965, with approximately one hundred eighty thousand American combat troops throughout the country, both sides were anxious to test their skills against the enemy.

The Viet Cong guerillas had already established many important bases all over South Vietnam. On the Van Tuong Peninsula that juts into the South China Sea, approximately fifteen thousand men of the elite First Viet Cong Regiment were encamped in a large fortified base. That was just twelve miles south of the important marine airstrip at Chu Lai. Then, on August 15, a Viet Cong deserter told the marines that the First Viet Cong Regiment was preparing an attack on Chu Lai. The marine commander ordered a strong preemptive strike.

In an extraordinary example of coordinated planning, the marines organized Operation Starlite in three days, the first major military action in Vietnam by U.S. combat forces. The highly complex, three-prong land, sea, and air attack utilized troops, air support, tanks, and naval gunfire. On land, marines would attack Chu Lai from the north. From the sky airborne troops would attack from three helicopter-landing zones—code-named "Red," "White," and "Blue"—located inland. From the sea, a marine unit would launch an amphibious assault from the South China Sea in the east.

On the morning of August 18, 1965, Operation Starlite was launched. Marines in amphibious landing craft shored on the beaches of the peninsula. Initially they encountered fierce resistance from the Viet Cong, but the marine attack was so swift and strong that the overwhelmed Viet Cong soon retreated in panic. Meanwhile, from the inland side, the marine airborne troops were engaged in a brutal firefight. Marines carried to landing zone Blue almost landed directly on top of five hundred surprised Viet Cong troops. As the Viet Cong regiment attempted to escape to the north, they ran headlong into the marine force advancing south from Chu Lai.

When Operation Starlite ended 6 days later, the First Viet Cong Regiment was effectively destroyed having officially suffered 614 killed in action. The marines lost forty-five men. The victory would heavily influence subsequent American operations.

Opposite: Viet Cong soldiers captured during Operation Starlite.

QUICK FACTS

- Fuel for helicopters and airplanes is measured by weight as well as gallons because weight affects the flying ability of the aircraft. In the Huey, a 200-gallon fuel tank weighs 1,200 pounds when full.

- Base camps and outposts used fortifications, known as "bunkers," for shelter and protection from attack. Bunker walls were composed of layers of sandbags. Each sandbag weighed an average of 60 pounds.

- Helicopters were used in search-and-rescue missions of downed pilots. One search-and-rescue helicopter was the Sikorsky CH-53B Sea Stallion. It was more popularly known by its two nicknames: "Super Jolly Green Giant" and "Buff," which stood for "big, ugly, fat fellow."

- Most troops arrived in Vietnam in airplanes. For many, the first memory of Vietnam was the "wall" of intense heat combined with the pungent smells of sweat, dung, rotting vegetation, food, and smoke that would hit them the moment they stepped out of an airplane's cabin.

Above: Helicopters on a mission in Vietnam.

The Vietnam War was the first to make widespread use of helicopters. These aerial, mechanical "horses" gave these twentieth-century cavalry troops mobility and battlefield firepower support that had never been seen before. A whole military doctrine was created for this new style of fighting called "airmobile operations."

Though planes were a part of airmobile operations, helicopters were the primary aircraft used. Helicopters could rapidly carry troops to isolated areas and land in clearings too small or rugged for airplanes. They could also provide close, hovering, treetop-level fire support against enemy positions, and quick evacuation of the wounded. The U.S. forces employed twenty types of helicopters in the Vietnam War. The workhorse of the group was the Bell UH-1H Iroquois, more popularly known as the Huey, which could be easily adapted to the roles needed. As troop transports, known as "slicks," the Huey carried troops and supplies. Gunships, known as "cobras," had extra machine guns and cannon. "Medivacs" were designed to quickly transport wounded from the battlefield. Command ships had extra communications equipment and were used by commanders flying over a battlefield.

Airmobile operations freed troops from being tied to road networks or waterways that could be cut off by the enemy. Even if an American unit was surrounded and was fighting a superior enemy force, it was not totally isolated. Because of the unique mobility of helicopters, they could swoop in at a moment's notice and provide additional firepower or troop reinforcements. U.S. Army General William DuPuy explained, "[F]rom the first shot [fired] and every minute thereafter the advantage turned in our favor because the Viet Cong or the NVA were seldom able to reinforce . . . But every minute we were able to bring in fighters, attack helicopters, artillery, and additional troops by helicopter."

Helicopters were the primary air arms of the army and marines, but not of the air force. Air Force Captain Bruce Wallace witnessed the use of gunships against the enemy. He said, "It is always an experience for an air force pilot to watch a gaggle of Hueys attack a target. . . . In [an air force jet squadron] attack, the target is always in front of us. Not so with a Huey. To watch four or eight of them at a time maneuvering up and down and laterally and even backward boggles a fighter pilot's mind. Those guys swarm a target like bees over honey."

Opposite: Huey helicopters in action.

QUICK FACTS

- Joe Galloway, a reporter for United Press International, was awarded the Bronze Star Medal with a Combat V for rescuing wounded soldiers under fire during the battle at Ia Drang. It was a rare honor; few civilians ever receive military decorations.

- To make it easy to understand radio message communication, the military uses the phonetic alphabet, which is: Alpha, Bravo, Charlie, Delta, Echo, Fox-trot, Golf, Hotel, India, Juliet, Kilo, Lima, Mike, November, Oscar, Papa, Quebec, Romeo, Sierra, Tango, Uniform, Victor, Whiskey, X-Ray, Yankee, Zulu.

- Steel helmets had many uses beyond protecting a soldier's head. Upended helmets filled with hot water would be used as wash basins for cleaning and shaving, or for cooking.

Above: U.S. soldiers advance into a part of the Ia Drang River valley that has just been hit by bombs from a B-52 bombing mission.

In 1965 American military support to South Vietnam was dramatically expanding. American combat troops were entering South Vietnam in force. The North Vietnamese government realized that it had to move quickly and decisively to win the war while there were still relatively few American troops in South Vietnam.

They decided to attack the strategically important region of Central Highlands, South Vietnam. If the North Vietnamese Army could seize control of this area, South Vietnam would be cut into two and thus be easy prey for a quick conquest. Through intelligence sources, Gen. Westmoreland learned of their plan and ordered his airmobile cavalry units to seek out and destroy the enemy before it could launch the campaign. Lieutenant Colonel Harold G. Moore's battalion was one of the units that participated in the Ia Drang campaign, named after a river in the Central Highlands. On the morning of November 14, 1965, he and an advance echelon of his men disembarked from their Hueys at a site in the Central Highlands. Moore and his men barely had time to establish a defensive perimeter—a ring of armed guards to protect the landing site—before they came under fierce attack. Lt. Herrick's platoon became isolated and surrounded. What they later discovered was that they had landed in the middle of sixteen hundred North Vietnamese Army troops.

Intense fighting continued throughout the day and into the evening. The following morning the men under Moore's command faced disaster. The enemy had broken through a portion of the perimeter. Lieutenant Charles Hastings, the forward air controller whose job was to coordinate all air support, immediately got on the radio. He later said, "I used the code word 'Broken Arrow,' which meant 'American unit in contact and in danger of being overrun,' and we received all available aircraft in South Vietnam for close air support. We had aircraft stacked at one-thousand-foot intervals from seven thousand feet to thirty-five thousand feet." Bombs and machine-gun fire from these aircraft, along with artillery shelling, helped save Lt. Col. Moore and his men. The Ia Drang campaign would continue until November 26. When it concluded, the American operation had successfully spoiled the North Vietnamese Army's attempt to seize the Central Highlands. Even so, the North Vietnamese learned many important lessons about fighting Americans, especially that U.S. superiority in the air and with artillery could be neutralized by close-quarters—hand-to-hand—fighting.

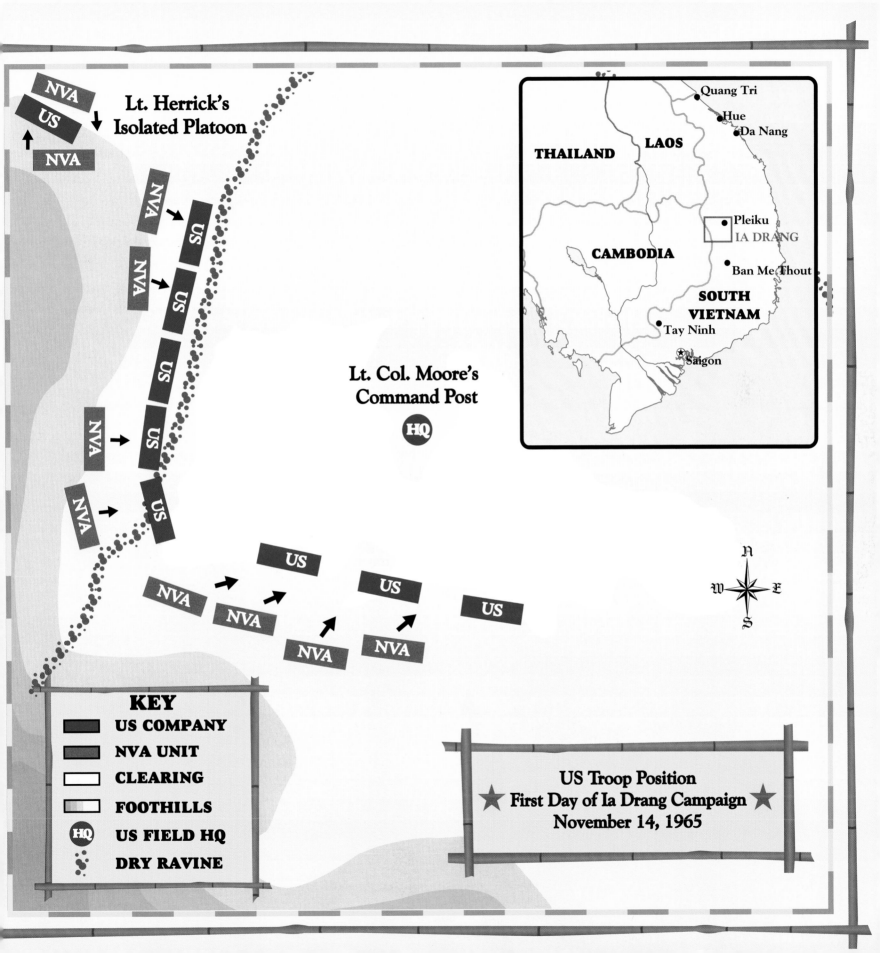

NVA

US

Lt. Herrick's
Isolated Platoon

NVA

NVA → US

NVA → US

US

US

US

NVA → US

NVA → US

Lt. Col. Moore's
Command Post

HQ

US

US

NVA → →

NVA →

NVA → US

NVA → US

NVA

Inset map:

Quang Tri

Hue

Da Nang

THAILAND **LAOS**

Pleiku
IA DRANG

CAMBODIA

Ban Me Thout

**SOUTH
VIETNAM**

Tay Ninh

⭐ Saigon

N
W + E
S

KEY

▮	**US COMPANY**
▮	**NVA UNIT**
▢	**CLEARING**
▢	**FOOTHILLS**
HQ	**US FIELD HQ**
⁝	**DRY RAVINE**

⭐ **US Troop Position**
First Day of Ia Drang Campaign ⭐
November 14, 1965

- The first Australian force in South Vietnam arrived in 1962. It was called the Australian Army Training Team Vietnam and was composed of 30 men expertly trained in jungle warfare. Their mission was to assist in training South Vietnamese Army troops in jungle warfare methods.

- The first New Zealand force was an administrative unit that helped the South Vietnamese government. It arrived in 1964. Three years later the first combat infantry unit arrived. Because there were so few New Zealand troops in Vietnam, a combined Australian/New Zealand force was created and called the Australian and New Zealand Army Corps (ANZAC).

- New Zealand troops were referred to as the "Kiwi Infantry," after New Zealand's national bird. By the end of the war, New Zealand suffered 83 men killed in action.

- The Australian and New Zealand troops traditionally celebrate the end of a mission with a barbecue.

Above: A unit of Royal Australian Air Force troops disembarking from an airplane at Tan Son Nhut airport, Saigon.

From 1965 to 1972, the United States supplied most of the combat forces in Vietnam and did most of the fighting in the country. But they did not fight alone. In order to get international support for America's involvement in the Vietnam War, President Johnson made an official call for "free world military forces" to forge an alliance of "many flags" to fight the Communists. A total of forty countries answered President Johnson's call and sent support into Vietnam. The most significant military support came from Australia, New Zealand, and South Korea.

Australia became involved because it was concerned that a Communist Vietnam would threaten democracies throughout Southeast Asia, particularly Indonesia, which is very close to the northern coast of Australia. New Zealand, though farther away, sent troops for the same reason. South Korea sent troops because of its recent, bitter experience with Communist invasion by the North Korean Army during the Korean War.

The Australian forces were stationed in Phuoc Tuy Province just southeast of Saigon. With their aggressive patrolling, they soon became a major threat to Viet Cong in the area.

The top Communist leadership in the province decided to "teach the Australians a lesson," one that would also send a message to local villagers. That lesson began on August 17, 1966, and was called the Battle of Long Tan. Australian patrols suddenly found themselves ambushed by large concentrations of Viet Cong, who repeatedly struck at the outnumbered Australians.

Private Harry Esler remembered thinking during one attack that "[i]t was just like a kangaroo shoot. They were coming in waves. They were blowing bugles off to the left, in front, and across to the right. I remember thinking, 'I wish I had a set of bagpipes here. I'd put the fear of [the Lord] up those blokes!'"

Despite the odds, the Australians refused to give up. The fighting continued throughout the day and into the evening. The following day, the Australians discovered a battlefield littered with enemy dead.

The lesson the Viet Cong had attempted to teach the Australians had cost them 245 men. The Australians suffered only seventeen dead and nineteen wounded. It was a humiliating defeat for the Viet Cong.

Opposite: A South Vietnamese Marine leads a patrol through a flooded rice paddy field.

● To stop North Vietnamese Army (NVA) infiltration across the DMZ, the United States launched Operation Die Marker, an attempt to construct a 25-mile-long high-tech anti-infiltration barrier cleared of all vegetation and containing barbed wire, minefields, watchtowers, and state-of-the-art electronic devices, including sensors that detected movement and sound along the DMZ. Troops called it "McNamara's Wall," after U.S. Secretary of Defense Robert S. McNamara. The barrier was never finished.

● The North Vietnamese Army logistics staff made elaborate calculations of load capacities and travel distances for supplies from North Vietnam to various base camps in the south. Some of the figures were: a man traveling over easy terrain could transport 55 pounds of rice, or 33 to 44 pounds of arms and munitions, approximately 15.5 miles during a day, or 12.4 miles at night. In mountainous or hilly terrain, the load was 28 pounds of rice, or 27 to 33 pounds of munitions, and the distance was 9 miles during a day, or 7.5 miles at night. A buffalo cart could transport 770 pounds of supplies 7.5 miles per day. A horse cart could transport 473 pounds 12.4 miles per day.

The two most important man-made land features in the Vietnam War were the Ho Chi Minh Trail and the Demilitarized Zone—the DMZ.

The Ho Chi Minh Trail was the name for an elaborate system of roads, depots, and rest areas and was the main supply route from North Vietnam into South Vietnam for Communist troops. The trail was primarily in the neutral countries of Laos and Cambodia—a clear violation of those countries' neutrality. Neither Laos nor Cambodia wanted to join the war. But while the Cambodian government tried to stay politically neutral, the government of Laos was openly sympathetic to the Communist cause. Therefore, as long as the North Vietnamese used the trail to transport troops and supplies for fighting in South Vietnam and not to attack Laos or Cambodia, those countries did nothing to stop the illegal use of their territory.

The Ho Chi Minh Trail was of enormous strategic advantage for the Communists. The border between North and South Vietnam was only thirty-nine miles long. In comparison the Ho Chi Minh Trail in 1963 was more than six hundred miles long. Thanks to the trail, the Communists could attack South Vietnam from anywhere along its western border. MACV recognized this and did everything it could, both officially and covertly, to destroy the trail and cut off supplies. Though it had occasional successes, they were only temporary. By 1971 the network would grow to contain approximately two thousand seven hundred roads and trails.

The Demilitarized Zone, the other important feature, was created at the 1954 Geneva Peace Conference between the French and the Viet Minh. It was an approximately five-mile-wide neutral "buffer" zone along the 17th parallel in about the middle of Vietnam that was supposed to be a temporary border between North and South Vietnam. As part of the terms of the peace treaty, signed in 1956, military troops or activity were forbidden in the DMZ. But that neutrality was violated repeatedly by North Vietnam throughout the Vietnam War. As a result, the South Vietnamese side of the boundary became a heavily defended region.

Opposite: A marine crouches in a pagoda entrance in a village near the DMZ.

QUICK FACTS

- The U.S government's General Accounting Office (GAO) did a study to see how much Operation Rolling Thunder cost. It totaled all the American expenses—including aircrew salaries, maintenance of the airplanes, the cost of the bombs, and so on—and compared it to an estimate of the value of the North Vietnamese property damaged or destroyed. The GAO calculated that in 1967 alone, the United States spent an average of $9.60 to inflict $1.00 worth of damage.

- Navy Lieutenant Commander John McCain, a bomber pilot on the aircraft carrier *Oriskany*, was one of the many pilots who flew a Rolling Thunder mission. He would later be shot down and spend the rest of the Vietnam War as a prisoner of war. After he was freed he entered politics, eventually becoming a U.S. senator from Arizona and a presidential candidate.

- During the Vietnam War, U.S. Air Force bombers and fighter-bombers dropped an estimated 6.2 million tons of bombs. This amount, which does not include bombs dropped by U.S. Navy, Marine Corps, and South Vietnamese aircraft, was almost 3 times the 2.2 million tons of bombs dropped in World War II.

Above: Air Force F-105 Thunderchiefs refueling during a mission.

President Johnson believed that once the North Vietnamese saw the buildup of American military power in South Vietnam, they would agree to end the war and let South Vietnam remain a separate and independent nation. But this was not the case. Despite an increase in military aid and combat troops, North Vietnam was consistently able to send men and supplies south.

One man who claimed he had an answer that would solve President Johnson's problem was Air Force Chief of Staff General Curtis LeMay. LeMay had repeatedly told President Johnson that if his squadrons were allowed to conduct an all-out bombing campaign against North Vietnam, he could bomb the country "back to the Stone Age."

President Johnson refused to go all-out because he wanted to keep civilian casualties to a minimum. But he did like the idea of using air power to try to compel the North Vietnamese to ask for peace. On March 2, 1965, the first mission under Operation Rolling Thunder was launched against an ammunition depot just north of the Demilitarized Zone in North Vietnam. Unlike bombing campaigns in other wars in which the military leaders chose the targets and scheduled the attacks, President Johnson and his advisors strictly controlled what would be bombed and when and how often.

Operation Rolling Thunder would continue off and on for the next three years, striking bridges and transportation routes, industrial centers, ammunition dumps, and petroleum centers. In all, about 643,000 tons—1.3 billion pounds—of bombs were dropped. Despite this massive number, and the vast destruction it caused, Operation Rolling Thunder was a failure. After every air raid, the North Vietnamese were able to quickly repair the damage, so delays of transporting men and supplies were minor. The result was a big boost in North Vietnamese morale. Ton That Tung, a North Vietnamese civilian, said, "The Americans thought that the more bombs they dropped, the quicker we would fall to our knees and surrender. But the bombs heightened rather than dampened our spirit."

In fact U.S. intelligence gathering discovered that the North Vietnamese were able to adapt so well to the attacks that the flow of supplies actually *increased.*

Opposite: An air force bombing mission over North Vietnam.

QUICK FACTS

- Search-and-destroy missions such as Operation Cedar Falls were usually named after American cities. Cedar Falls is a city in Iowa. Others included Operation El Paso (I and II), Operation Irving, Operation Macon, and Operation Junction City.

- Operation Cedar Falls saw the first major use of a gigantic earthmover known as the "Rome Plow." Nicknamed "hogjaws," these were 60-ton earthmoving tractors built with a specially curved blade that could splinter tree trunks 3 feet in diameter. They were named after Rome, Georgia, where they were manufactured.

- The M-16 assault rifle was designed for right-handed people. When a left-handed soldier fired it, the hot brass shells ejected across the face and body, instead of away from it. Sometimes one of these hot shells would fly down a soldier's collar.

Above: American soldiers attacking Viet Cong snipers.

The Viet Cong had many base camps scattered throughout the rural areas of South Vietnam. One of the most notorious was called "the Iron Triangle," located just twenty miles north of the South Vietnamese capital city of Saigon. In a heavily forested, sparsely populated region, the Viet Cong developed a sanctuary complete with an elaborate tunnel system that stretched for miles. From the Iron Triangle, the Viet Cong would stage terrorist raids on Saigon and other nearby populated regions.

On January 8, 1967, American forces under the command of Major General William DuPuy launched Operation Cedar Falls in an attempt to break the Viet Cong's grip on the region. More than thirty thousand American and South Vietnamese troops participated, making it the largest campaign at the time. Using a "hammer and anvil" approach, airmobile units, acting as the "hammer," dropped onto the northern edge of the Iron Triangle and advanced south. At the same time, combined American and South Vietnamese forces established themselves along the southern border of the Iron Triangle. Any enemy troops attempting to escape south would thus run into this "anvil."

Included in the operation was a forced resettlement plan to relocate villagers that American troops found. The purpose was to deny the Viet Cong assistance and supplies that villages in the region habitually provided. Villagers were told to leave their ancestral land and most of their property. They were allowed to take what they could carry, and the roads were filled with families and livestock heading to their new homes. Army General Bernard Rogers later recalled, "It was to be expected that uprooting these villagers would evoke resentment, and it did."

A third goal of the operation was the location and destruction of the Viet Cong tunnel system in the area. On January 18, American troops achieved that mission's goal, discovering a tunnel complex that contained thousands of important documents. The complex was so large it took four days to explore it fully.

The intelligence material gathered amounted to more than five hundred thousand pages of documents. Lieutenant General Jonathan Seaman called the discovery "the biggest intelligence breakthrough of the war."

When Operation Cedar Falls concluded on January 26, Maj. Gen. DuPuy claimed that it was "a blow from which the VC in this area may never recover." Though the Viet Cong suffered a major setback, not long after the Americans left, they returned and soon were back in control of the area.

Opposite: Bamboo huts go up in flames during an effort by U.S. Army infantrymen to completely level the Viet Cong stronghold of Ben Suc during Operation Cedar Falls.

Above: South Vietnamese troops using sampans for transport during a patrol.

South Vietnam has more than three thousand miles of navigable rivers, canals, and waterways, as well as twelve hundred miles of coastline. Because South Vietnam's road system was so primitive, these water routes were used much the same way highways are in the United States. Control of the rivers and coastline was vital in order to make sure food, supplies, and people could freely travel through South Vietnam. The battle for control of the coastline and inland waterways was called the Riverine War.

Most of the inland navigable channels were in the vast Mekong Delta. This twenty-six-thousand-square-mile region was home to most of the South Vietnamese and was also one of the largest rice-growing regions in the world. The Viet Cong had been infiltrating the area since the war with the French in the nineteen fifties. By the time the Americans arrived in force in the mid-sixties, the Viet Cong controlled most of the Mekong Delta. Though every American service participated in the Riverine War, it was primarily fought by the U.S. Navy. Two important campaigns in the Riverine War were Operation Market Time, which focused on Communist boat traffic on the northern coast of South Vietnam, and Operation Game Warden, which focused on the rivers and canals.

One of the most dangerous Viet Cong strongholds in the Mekong Delta was the Rung Sat—the "Forest of Assassins." In October 1966, Boatswain's Mate First Class James E. Williams was leading a two-boat canal patrol into the Rung Sat as part of a mission of Operation Game Warden. During their patrol they encountered two sampans—wide, flat-bottomed boats—carrying Communist troops. Williams ordered pursuit when the sampans attempted to escape. When Williams's two boats—carrying a total of eight men and armed only with machine guns—rounded a bend in the canal, they were shocked to discover a convoy of sampans and junks carrying about one thousand armed North Vietnamese troops! Williams hesitated only a second before ordering an attack. Charging forward at full throttle, Williams's tiny force slalomed through and over the enemy ships, all of their machine guns blazing. Williams then called in Huey gunships for support. When the three-hour battle was over, it was estimated that the North Vietnamese had lost more than one thousand men and sixty-five vessels. The Americans received minor damage to their boats, and two men were slightly wounded. For his extraordinary action, Williams was awarded the Medal of Honor.

Opposite: A U.S. Navy river patrol–boat crewman during a pass down one of South Vietnam's rivers.

QUICK FACTS

● The Marine Corps conducted a comparative study between Force Recon and regular marine units to judge their effectiveness. One part of the study noted that, with regular infantry units, the enemy initiated contact 80 percent of the time. But Force Recon turned the tables by initiating contact in 95 percent of its engagements.

● Wayne E. Rollings was an extraordinarily fit marine. On April 1, 1975, he set the record for nonstop, continuous-motion, hands-behind-the-head, straight-legged, elbow-touching-opposite-knee sit-ups. After 15 hours and 32 minutes, he had completed a total of 35,000 sit-ups.

● The house of a rural Vietnamese peasant was called a "hooch" by U.S. troops, who also used the nickname for the tent, bunker, or building that was their own personal quarters.

● The reason the special-operations units are known as "elite" units is because they are few in number and highly trained. On the average less than 5 percent of the applicants qualify for the special-operations training program. Of that group, an average of only 3 out of 10 successfully complete the training.

Above: A ranger applies camouflage face paint prior to going on patrol.

From the very beginning of the war, American military leaders recognized that conventional military tactics alone would not achieve victory in Vietnam. Specially trained men operating in small teams deep behind enemy lines were necessary in order to gather intelligence; conduct observation for accurate air strikes, artillery barrages, and ambushes; and head other counterinsurgency missions.

This unconventional war of "carrying the battle to the enemy where he least expected it" was performed by elite special-operations units from each branch of the military. The army had the Special Forces—popularly called the Green Berets after their distinctive headgear. The marines had Force Recon. The navy had the SEALs—for Sea, Air, Land—and the air force had the Air Commandos.

All special-operations volunteers go through rigorous training that is capped by an extraordinarily grueling seven-day test of intelligence, character, strength, and stamina known as "Hell Week." Recalling one part of the training, Navy SEAL Robert Gormly said, "Everywhere we went that week we had to carry our eleven-man rubber rafts that [seemed to] weigh at least a ton. One of [our instructor's] favorite tricks was to . . . jump up into one of the boats as we were running down the road . . . He'd stand up in the boat like Ben-Hur in the chariot, yelling at us to hurry up."

First Lieutenant Wayne E. Rollings led a number of Force Recon teams in Vietnam. These teams averaged four to six men. One intelligence-gathering mission demonstrated the high level of infiltration skills possessed by Force Recon members. Leading a team code-named "Grim Reaper," Rollings and his men entered enemy-held territory at night and quietly infiltrated an enemy outpost. For the next several hours they conducted a thorough search, counting 364 North Vietnamese Army troops in the outpost, as well as the location of the enemy fortifications. After their search, the Grim Reapers withdrew to a safe location without the enemy discovering them. Rollings then radioed an air strike that destroyed the complex.

The intelligence-gathering value of these special-operations teams was acknowledged by Marine General Raymond Davis. "Our most reliable intelligence came from small four- or six- man patrols. . . . As a result we knew with some precision where the enemy was located, what he was doing, and just as important, what he was not."

Opposite: A U.S. Special Forces officer shouts instructions to his command composed of native Montagnard tribesmen.

QUICK FACTS

- There are two types of officers in the military services—those who attend universities or military academies and receive their commissions after successfully graduating, thereafter known as "officers," and those who are promoted from the enlisted ranks. Officers who were promoted from the enlisted ranks were known as "mustangs," after the wild, untamed horse of the American West. Enlisted men generally liked these officers because they had once been "one of them" and were thus more sensitive to their needs.

- American soldiers and marines in the Vietnam War were known as "grunts." This was inspired by the sound they made as they shouldered their heavy rucksacks onto their backs.

The Vietnam War is sometimes referred to as the "company commanders' war" because so many of the battles fought were small-unit actions of forty people or fewer. The North Vietnamese Army and the Viet Cong preferred to stage hit-and-run raids and would only engage in open battles if they were trapped or had an overwhelming force.

Casualty rates were high among the lieutenants and captains who commanded the platoons and companies—almost four times that of officers with the rank of major and above. Because of a rotation system that caused all but the most senior commanders to serve only one year in Vietnam, incoming junior officers were generally inexperienced—being "green"—in the art of combat. Once they successfully completed their tour in Vietnam, officers were no longer obligated to return. But if they wanted to return, they were allowed to volunteer. Some officers served three tours (three years) in Vietnam. Sergeants, the backbone of most armies, worked closely with the enlisted men and assisted in the training of new lieutenants and captains. Most sergeants would do what they could to pass on their experiences to officers who were often their junior in age as well as experience. Army Sergeant Al Fallow made this comment to his company commander: "There's the way it's taught, and the way it's done, and in combat, any similarity between the two is usually a matter of pure coincidence."

The most difficult period for a junior officer in his new combat command was the first few weeks. He had to quickly learn everything he could about the men in his command—who was reliable, who was lazy, who was the best scout, and so on. And he had to learn—immediately—all the combat survival skills unique to the Vietnam War, particularly regarding the Viet

Above: Wounded servicemen arriving from Vietnam at Andrews Air Force Base.

Opposite: After a battle, soldiers await the arrival of helicopters that will return them to base. At their feet is the body of a fallen comrade.

Cong booby traps. If he did not, he could quickly become a casualty himself. Usually by the time an officer gained sufficient experience, he was nearing the end of his tour—referred to as being a "short" or "short-timer"—and would soon be reassigned elsewhere. Some officers volunteered to do additional tours in Vietnam, but most did not.

The best officers always put the concerns of their men first. Sometimes that concern extended beyond the men under their command. Chief Warrant Officer Bruce McInnes, an army helicopter pilot, was asked by his platoon leader, Captain Roy Ferguson, to help him out on a mission of mercy to the Vinh-Son Orphanage and School, a local orphanage containing more than twelve hundred children and was run by a group of Catholic nuns. In a letter McInnes wrote home to his mother, he said, in part:

"[The kids] just went wild when they saw us. And no wonder—for the past five months, Capt. Ferguson . . . has been practically their only link with the life of clothing, toys, and personal American friendship. They've adopted him, in their own way, as a sort of godfather. . . . Capt. Ferguson will be leaving soon, and I will sort of assume the privilege of being the go-between for these children and the assistance that comes in. . . . These kids aren't underprivileged—they're nonprivileged, and they're running. Running toward a way of life where they can better themselves on their own. But they're so young, we have to help them to walk before we let them run. . . . There's no law here requiring children to attend school. They go because they are hungry for knowledge and because their stomachs are hungry. An education can change that, and we must help them get that education. . . . Send *anything* that might be useful to [the orphanage] care of myself . . . And don't be surprised if the next piece of mail you get from Vietnam is a thank-you note from some very, very grateful Vietnamese youngster."

Opposite: A soldier who has counted off his days remaining in Vietnam.

EFT
VIET-NAM
APRIL
MAY
JUNE
JULY
AUGUST
SEPTEMBER
NOVEMBER
DECEMBER
JANUARY
FEBUARY
545

QUICK FACTS

- In the Pentagon and among senior military commanders in Vietnam, the war was known as "Westy's War" because of Westmoreland's important role in developing the strategy and tactics used from 1965 to mid-1968.

- Giap could be icy calm one moment and erupt into a violent tirade the next. This extreme contrast in behavior caused his contemporaries to give him the nickname "Nue Lua"—the "Volcano Under the Snow."

- Ironically Giap's only formal military training came from the Americans. During World War II, he was trained in guerilla warfare in an American camp in China.

- *Time* magazine named Westmoreland "Man of the Year" for 1965.

Above: Vo Nguyen Giap, defense minister of North Vietnam and its top general.

The two most famous military leaders in the Vietnam War were Gen. William C. Westmoreland of the U.S. Army, and Gen. Vo Nguyen Giap of North Vietnam. In the history of warfare it would be difficult to find two opponents who were so different. The only things they had in common were that they both were well educated and were passionately committed to the service of their countries.

Westmoreland had ancestors who fought in the American Revolution and the American Civil War. A graduate of the U.S. Military Academy at West Point and a decorated veteran of both World War II and the Korean War, Westmoreland assumed command of the ground forces in Vietnam with the confidence of a man who had successfully waged war. He regarded his post at MACV, which he took command of in 1964 at the age of sixty, as the high point of his military career. He was determined to quickly win the war.

Giap was a high school history teacher who was self-taught in the art of war. As a teacher Giap gained a reputation as a lecturer of military history. He was appointed the commanding general of the Viet Minh troops in 1945 at the age of thirty-four and became their foremost military commander during the war with the French in the early 1950s. His crowning achievement was his decisive victory over the French at Dien Bien Phu in 1954. Giap was made the commander in chief of the North Vietnamese Army and later became minister of defense in the North Vietnamese government.

Giap joined the Communist Party in 1937. In 1939 the French government outlawed the Communist Party in France and its colonies, forcing members to either flee to other countries or go into hiding. Giap went into exile in China. But his wife, baby daughter, and his wife's sister were captured by the French security forces in Vietnam and thrown into prison. There, Giap's sister-in-law was guillotined, and his wife was later beaten to death by the guards. Giap's daughter also died in prison, the cause of which is unknown. Their deaths reaffirmed Giap's commitment to fight for an independent Vietnam.

When American combat troops arrived in 1965, Giap used the same tactics he had perfected against the French. Unfortunately for him the Americans were more powerful, and Giap's efforts never achieved the same military success on the battlefield.

Opposite: Gen. Westmoreland.

QUICK FACTS

- One of the most versatile fighter-bombers in the Vietnam War was the F-4 Phantom jet. It served on navy aircraft carriers. In the air force, it served as a fighter, fighter bomber, a reconnaissance plane, and other roles.

- A second U.S. fleet, named Task Force 77, operated from a second location, about 90 miles off the coast of South Vietnam. This location was called "Dixie Station."

- The nickname for the Seventh Fleet when it was at Yankee Station was the "Tonkin Gulf Yacht Club."

During the war, the U.S. Seventh Fleet was responsible for ocean-based operations against North Vietnam. Aircraft carriers of the Seventh Fleet launched attacks about eighty-six miles off the coast of North Vietnam in the international waters of the Tonkin Gulf. This location was called "Yankee Station." Navy air missions targeted a wide variety of sites, including road and rail networks, depots and munitions factories, power plants, and troop centers.

Because North Vietnam did not have any submarines, battleships, cruisers, or destroyers, the Seventh Fleet was relatively safe from enemy attack. But carrier operations are still dangerous, especially during wartime. Navy pilot Lieutenant Commander John McCain was involved in one of the worst carrier accidents in the Vietnam War. It happened on the USS *Forrestal* in 1967. He was sitting in the cockpit of his plane, waiting to take off, when it happened. He later wrote, "I was third in line on the port side of the ship. . . . In the next instant, a Zuni missile struck the belly fuel tank of my plane, tearing it open, igniting two hundred gallons of fuel that spilled onto the deck and knocking two of my bombs to the deck. . . . Stray voltage from an electrical charge used to start the engine of a nearby F-4 Phantom, also waiting to take off, had somehow fired the six-foot Zuni from beneath the plane's wing."

Chaos erupted on the flight deck as the fire spread among the heavily armed planes. Young men eighteen and nineteen years of age fought to save the ship from the fire and exploding bombs and missiles. When it was over, the *Forrestal* had lost 134 men and more than 20 planes. Damage to the ship was so severe it had to leave Yankee Station for repairs.

Above: Crew members fighting fires on board USS *Forrestal* on July 29, 1967.

Opposite: The USS *Enterprise* in the Tonkin Gulf at Yankee Station.

QUICK FACTS

- Because the Viet Cong most often entered villages at night, villagers gave them the sinister nickname of the "night visitors."

- Though an exact figure will never be known, the lowest accepted figure for civilians killed in the Vietnam War is 415,000.

- The U.S. umbrella organization coordinating the efforts to gain the South Vietnamese villagers' support for the government was named Civil Operations and Revolutionary Development Support (CORDS). The staff of CORDS included military advisors, foreign-service officers, public- and rural-health nurses, and agricultural advisors. At its peak CORDS had a staff of almost 6,500 people.

- One method of eliminating the villagers' support of the Viet Cong was to physically relocate entire villages, removing them from regions dominated by the Viet Cong and placing them in new villages in government-controlled areas. Though it was successful in removing people, its success in gaining the villagers' support for the government was mixed because many of the new villages were fenced in with barbed wire and had guardposts, making them resemble large prison camps rather than new villages.

Securing the support and cooperation of the millions of rural peasants was an ongoing goal for both sides during the Vietnam War. Many villagers didn't care about the politics and would have preferred to be left alone to tend to their farms, rice paddies, and livestock. But they were realists. Whichever side had the power to protect them from threats of torture and death would be the side they would support. Support for the Communists took many forms ranging from enlisting in the Viet Cong or North Vietnamese Army, to acting as covert agents, to supplying rice and other food, to simply signaling the presence of American or South Vietnamese troops.

Le Ly, a fifteen-year-old village girl, was typical of Viet Cong sympathizers. She had a simple yet efficient system of signaling if any enemy troops were near. She always wore three shirts. "The top shirt—the one I would wear all day if nothing happened—was brown. Any Viet Cong seeing it would know things were clear in my sector. The second shirt was white, which I would show if anything suspicious had happened. . . . The bottom shirt . . . was all black and that meant a major threat. . . ."

Nguyen Duy, while still in his teens, had become one of the most famous poets in North Vietnam. He served in the North Vietnamese Army, and one of his tasks was to clean rifles. One day, while cleaning an AK-47, the standard assault rifle of the Communist forces, his colonel asked, "A beautiful weapon, don't you think?" Nguyen Duy replied, "There's nothing beautiful about it—it's just an instrument of war, and I don't think there's anything beautiful about war." He later recalled, "During the time I was serving in the army, my only wish was to return to [my] poor but peaceful village. When I came back after the war, everything had turned upside down. That peaceful beauty had vanished. . . . There is a line in one of my poems that goes, 'In the end, in every war, whoever won, the people always lost.'"

American troops entering South Vietnam found themselves confronting an enemy physically indistinguishable from the people they were supposed to defend. Because of the difficulty in positively identifying a guerilla Viet Cong member, an attitude began to develop during a campaign or a mission that, "If it's dead and it's Vietnamese, it's VC." Lieutenant Vincent Okamoto,

Opposite: A young Vietnamese boy carried in a basket by a U.S. paratrooper.

a Japanese American, recalled that because of his Asian features, "I was nearly killed by Americans who mistook me for a Vietnamese." Okamoto participated in the Phoenix Program, an operation designed to eliminate the network of local Viet Cong agents and supporters. Periodically his superior officers would hand him a list of suspected individuals. He recalled, "The problem was, how do you find [them]? It's not like you had their address and telephone number. The normal procedure would be to go into a village and just grab someone and say, 'Where's Nguyen so-and-so?' Half the time the people were so afraid they would say anything." After they got the information they needed, he said, "Then that night [a Phoenix team] would come back, knock on the door [of the suspect's house]. . . . Whoever answered the door would get [killed]. As far as [the team was] concerned, whoever answered was a Communist."

Gen. Westmoreland called America's effort to rally villagers and pacify known Viet Cong–controlled hamlets "winning the hearts and minds." Many programs were run under this effort. One of the most effective was the Marine Corps' Combined Action Platoon, or CAP.

Marines realized that if they were to truly win the hearts and minds of the peasants, they'd have to provide around-the-clock security against the Viet Cong. To do so the marines stationed live-in forces generally consisting of a squad of marines, a corpsman, and a platoon of South Vietnamese local troops in villages—ideally some soldiers from the village itself. As much as possible, the marines would become members of the village.

Marine Sergeant James D. White was a member of the CAP assigned to the village of Binh Nighia. Shortly after his tour of duty in Vietnam was finished, and he was rotated home, his mother received a letter from Ho Chi, the school teacher in Binh Nighia. It read in part:

"[Sgt. White] is a good friend a lot of people like very much. He has done a number one job. For our people I want to thank you for having a number one son. About three months ago my village was having trouble with Viet Cong and Sgt. J. D. White and [squad] help protect my people and land. I want to thank him very much for helping have peace in my village. . . .

"I wish in my heart that every man was like him. . . .

"I hope some day we will all have peace and Charity."

Above: South Vietnamese villagers.

Opposite: Girl volunteers of the South Vietnamese People's Self-Defense Force.

QUICK FACTS

- A "million-dollar wound" was a wound serious enough to have a person shipped home but not serious enough to permanently cripple.

- The code word for corpsman was "Angel."

- U.S. forces suffered 47,382 killed in action and 153,303 wounded in action during the Vietnam War. Of those killed, 65.8 percent were army, 25.5 percent were marine, 4.3 percent were navy, 4.3 percent were air force, and 0.1 percent were coast guard personnel. Broken down by rank, 88.8 percent were enlisted men and warrant officers, 8.6 percent were lieutenants and captains, and 2.6 percent were majors and colonels. Twelve U.S. generals died in Vietnam.

- Estimates of South Vietnamese Army casualties vary. The lowest estimate is 110,357 killed in action and 499,026 wounded.

Above: A Huey with a red cross, signifying that it is an unarmed medical helicopter.

orpsmen, or medics—enlisted men trained to provide first aid on the battlefield—were vitally important to a combat unit. The medical help they gave to wounded men often meant the difference between life and death. The efforts of the corpsmen and medics, combined with quick helicopter evacuations known as "dustoffs," considerably lowered the death rate among U.S. combat casualties. The enemy recognized how important they were to a unit and specifically targeted them. Lee Reynolds, an army corpsman, said, "The VC were paid an incentive to kill a medic."

Corpsmen were among the most fearless men in combat. During a firefight, they could be seen crawling or rushing to help wounded men, heedless of the danger to themselves. Ralph Daniello was a navy corpsman assigned to a marine unit at Khe Sanh. Of his experience he later recalled, "I remember going through firefights, getting hit, and taking care of the wounded, and your hands are full of blood, and you wipe them off on your pants. After days and weeks of wearing the same clothes, your pants are still stiff from the blood."

Wayne Smith was an army combat medic. He later recalled, "Combat was horrible, but there was a beautiful side as well—the brotherhood between black soldiers and white soldiers and Hispanics and Native Americans. When we were in combat, all that mattered was trying to survive together. . . . In combat all that matters is: Are you going to do your duty and [help me] when I get hit? . . . I was eighteen and knew a little about how to save lives. . . ." His skills were put to the test during one operation in the Plain of Reeds near the Cambodian border. One of the soldiers tripped a booby trap called a "daisy chain"—a series of grenades strung together. Smith rushed forward to save the wounded. One soldier had one of the worst battlefield wounds possible—a punctured lung that produces what's called a "sucking chest" wound. He managed to save the life of that soldier. He later said, "If you don't panic, it's not hard, but you always have that fear of [making a mistake] and causing someone to die. There's nothing worse than that for a medic."

Thanks to the high quality of training that medics and corpsmen received, the mortality rate for wounded was, when compared to prior wars, an astonishingly low 1 to 2.5 percent, the lowest rate ever.

Opposite: Marines carrying a wounded comrade to a helicopter "dustoff" site.

QUICK FACTS

- The average age of American nurses in South Vietnam was 23.

- In addition to the responsibilities they had over others' lives, nurses faced constant danger themselves. Unlike other wars, which had established fighting areas (front lines, or the front) and combat-free rest areas (the rear), the Vietnam War was a guerilla war, meaning the whole country was a battle zone.

- First Lieutenant Sharon Lane was killed during a Viet Cong rocket attack on the hospital where she was stationed. She was the only nurse killed by enemy fire in the Vietnam War. In addition to receiving the Bronze Star posthumously, a statue of her by John Worthing was dedicated in her hometown of Canton, Ohio. In total, 8 U.S. military women died in the line of duty in the war.

- Most of the women who served in Vietnam were nurses. Approximately 160 women from all branches served in administrative positions, including clerical, intelligence, security, supply, data processing, and law enforcement. These were based in Saigon and Long Binh.

When wounded soldiers arrived for treatment at hospitals in South Vietnam, they were sometimes met with a sight they did not expect: an American woman in uniform. An estimated five thousand to six thousand American military nurses served in the Vietnam War.

Nurses in South Vietnam were given more responsibility than their stateside counterparts—making critical on-the-spot trauma decisions that otherwise would have been made by doctors, particularly if a large number of wounded arrived from a battle. As a result many received crash courses in advanced trauma and critical care. But for all of their valuable medical skill, wounded soldiers and marines received an invaluable morale boost simply from seeing a feminine American face in a distant, foreign, and hostile land. Lily Adams, a nurse who served in Vietnam, recalled, "They just wanted to hear the voice, smell the perfume. It would remind them of their girl-friends or wives. I had a strong [New York City] accent, and the guys from New York would just say, 'Keep on talking.'"

There were also unique risks to caring for wounded infantrymen. Nurse Adams recalled, "You had to wake these kids up by shaking their toes. You didn't want to be close enough that they would grab your neck and kill you. These were warriors . . . and their response was that of a warrior thinking he was getting attacked in the middle of his sleep."

In addition to wounded military personnel, military hospitals often cared for wounded civilians. All these civilians had additional health problems due to various tropical diseases, including intestinal worms. First Lieutenant Sharon

Lane wrote home about one such experience, "Two nights ago [I] was taking care of this eleven-year-old boy with a gunshot wound of the abdomen. . . . Just put a towel over him for a diaper and he had a huge, liquid BM [bowel movement]. Took it off and was washing it out in a pan of water and got this thing wrapped around my hand. Was about an eight-inch bowel worm. Nearly scared the BM out of me when [I] first saw it. Am now more cautious when washing out stuff like that."

Above, left: Nurses stationed at an evacuation hospital in South Vietnam.
Above, right: A nurse checking on a patient aboard a hospital ship off the coast of South Vietnam.

Opposite: An army nurse helping villagers during a Medical Civic Action Program (Medcap) visit.

QUICK FACTS

● In 1965 there were approximately 125 miles of tunnels in the area around Cu Chi, a village less than 20 miles northwest of Saigon.

● A number of inventions to find and destroy tunnels were created and tested. One device was a soil detector that, according to its inventors, could tell where tunnels were being dug. It weighed 106 pounds. The operator had to carry the heavy device on his back to a suspected tunnel site. Then he had to unstrap the device, set it up, and take his readings. The invention was called the Portable Differential Magnetometer (PDM), and it proved to be unreliable.

● German shepherds were also used in the tunnels to hunt Viet Cong. These dogs and their handlers received specific training and upon successful completion, were assigned mine, booby trap, and tunnel dog teams. These teams found more than 2,000 Viet Cong tunnels and bunkers.

Above: U.S. Marines searching tunnels in Da Nang for Viet Cong.

The Viet Cong were adept at creating havens and base camps throughout South Vietnam. As American troops soon discovered, these havens were not only in villages, forests, and mountains; they were underground as well.

The Viet Cong tunnel systems were elaborate underground complexes which, in some cases, extended for miles. They included storage areas, hospitals, kitchens, wells, sleeping chambers, firing bunkers, training areas—they were "cities" connected by underground roads.

Tran Thi Gung was a seventeen-year-old girl when she joined the Viet Cong in order to avenge the death of her father killed by South Vietnamese government troops. Of the tunnels she recalled, "When GIs discovered tunnel openings, they dynamited them, but the tunnels were so deep and had so many twists and turns, they couldn't do too much damage. It was like an underground maze. Most of the tunnels were just wide enough to crawl through. . . . Usually we didn't have to stay underground for more than a few hours at a time. . . . But one time I was stuck in a tunnel for seven days and seven nights while the Americans were constantly bombing us."

Volunteers who entered the tunnels to attack the Viet Cong were known as "tunnel rats." Like the Vietnamese, they were small, slender men. Their job was extremely risky. Armed only with a pistol and a flashlight, they would crawl through a dark tunnel searching for the enemy. They had to be wary of booby traps, dead ends, and ambushes. When they encountered the enemy, the firefight was short, fierce, and deafening in the confined area. As there was no place to retreat or hide, they had to shoot it out at point-blank range.

Tunnel rat C. W. Bowman recalled, "People asked me if I had a death wish: Why would anybody want to go down into the tunnel? I don't know. I was eighteen, and you're not going to die, at least you think you're not going to die. You're invincible. . . . It gets strange down there; it's quiet. It's cool, but the sweat is running off your body. . . . Your chest hurts because your heart is pounding so hard. . . . Your body sometimes feels like it's trying to tear itself in half. Part of it wants to go ahead because of the unknown, the challenge, but the other part, because of the fear and the unknown, wants to go back [to] where you came from."

Opposite: An infantryman being lowered into a Viet Cong tunnel.

QUICK FACTS

• Agent Blue was used against food crops. It was a water-soluble desiccant that prevented fruit or grain from forming without killing the plant itself.

• *Patches* was the name of one of the aircraft used on Operation Ranch Hand missions. It was one of the most rugged aircraft in the air force inventory. It flew for 10 years in Vietnam and was hit by enemy fire more than 600 times. It survived the war and is now on display at the U.S. Air Force Museum at Wright-Patterson Air Force Base in Dayton, Ohio.

• As a result of bombing and the use of herbicides in the war, which resulted in contamination and destruction of wildlife habitats in many areas, there are at least 21 species now on the endangered species list. They include the Tonkin snub-nosed monkey, the Malayan sun bear, the clouded leopard, the Vietnamese pheasant, and the Imperial pheasant.

• A reliable evaluation of the number of Vietnamese people affected by Agent Orange is almost impossible. But a team of Canadian experts conducted an independent study of the contaminated regions in the Alvoi Valley in 1999. Their findings revealed that children born in sprayed areas were more than 8 times as likely to suffer hernias and more than 3 times as likely to have cleft palates, be mentally retarded, and have extra fingers and toes.

Large areas of South Vietnam are covered in thick tropical vegetation ranging from dense forests, to tall elephant grass, to clinging vines troops called "wait-a-minute" vines (so named because anyone caught in them usually shouted "Wait a minute" as he fought to free himself). Such thick plant life offered countless places for Viet Cong forces to build sanctuaries, to hide, and to set up ambushes. To eliminate this cover, the U.S. military used herbicides in a defoliation-and-crop-destruction campaign code-named "Operation Ranch Hand."

While some herbicides were dispensed by riverboats, trucks, and men with individual sprayers, most were deployed by specially rigged helicopters or airplanes. The defoliants were named after the color of the stripes on their shipping containers. The active ingredient in all the herbicides was a poisonous substance called 2-, 3-, 7-, 8-tetrachlorodibenzo-para-dioxin (TCDD). The first used in South Vietnam were Agent Purple and Agent Pink. Later they were replaced with three others, one of which was Agent Orange.

Large tracts of land, particularly around base camps and other military installations, were laid barren of all plant life through the use of these herbicides. This made it much easier for American troops and aircraft to spot enemy movement. Ultimately approximately six million acres were sprayed by defoliants, destroying roughly ten percent of South Vietnam's forests. When Operation Ranch Hand concluded in 1970, approximately nineteen million gallons of herbicide had been used.

The defoliant campaign became controversial because of its impact on plants, animals, citizens, and soldiers, particularly the men who handled the herbicides. Over the years, health problems in people exposed to the herbicides, including respiratory problems, persistent skin rashes, some forms of skin cancer, and birth defects in their children, were widely reported. Numerous studies were conducted to track these complaints. The August 2003 issue of the *Journal of Occupational and Environmental Medicine*, which released the results of a 2002 study conducted in Bien Hoa City, reported high levels of dioxins in food and residents more than thirty years after the defoliant campaign had ended. Eventually chemical companies that manufactured the herbicides agreed to establish a trust fund of $180 million that would be distributed to veterans who suffered health problems or died as a result of exposure to the herbicides.

Opposite: An American airplane sprays defoliant over a region of South Vietnam.

QUICK FACTS

● Journalists would attend regular briefing meetings held by Military Assistance Command Office of Information (MACOI) every day at 5:00 P.M. Because the reporters distrusted the accuracy of the information presented by the military, the journalists called the briefings the "Five O'Clock Follies."

● Going on a patrol was just as dangerous for a journalist as it was for the sailors and troops. In the heat of battle everyone is a target. Freelance photographer/correspondent Dickey Chapelle was the first American female correspondent to be killed in action in Vietnam.

● The Vietnam War would establish the reputation of some of the greatest modern-print journalists in American history: David Halberstam of the *New York Times*; Joe Galloway and Neil Sheehan of United Press International; Peter Arnett of the Associated Press and, later, CNN; and Horst Faas, a photographer, among others.

Above: Newsmen killed in Saigon by Viet Cong guerrillas.

In the beginning of the Vietnam War, most news was told by reporters and photographers working for newspapers, magazines, or the syndicated wire services. Before the invention of modern conveniences such as fax machines and cell phones, writing and filing stories was a time-consuming task. Reports were filed through the government-controlled telegraph office, by courier, or sometimes by phone. Phones themselves were rare and unreliable. The Associated Press office in Saigon had only one phone—a battered, heavily taped device that was as priceless as it was fragile.

But as the war progressed, it was television journalism, then in its infancy, that came to dominate war reporting. The first television crews were at a great disadvantage compared to today's crews. Equipment was bulky, heavy, and by today's standards, crude. Crews of three men carried a camera that weighed as much as fifty pounds. Even so, ultimately, television's graphic, moving pictures of burning villages, dead bodies, blood-covered soldiers and civilians, and panic-stricken children would bring the war into Americans' living rooms. In the United States, the immediacy and the vividness of television reports would profoundly affect opinions about the war.

The quality of the journalists ranged from the brilliant to the totally ignorant. Pulitzer Prize–winner Eddie Adams noted once that "[y]ou had a lot of adventure seekers." In the most extreme cases Saigon-based journalists would rush to the battle scene invariably after it had ended, spend a few hours there, and then return to Saigon to file their stories.

Joe Galloway of United Press International was one of a handful of reporters who accompanied combat troops onto the field. Galloway was the only journalist who was with Lt. Col. Moore and his men during the Ia Drang campaign. At one point during the fighting, Galloway recalled, "The incoming fire was only a couple of feet off the ground, and I was down as flat as I could get when I felt the toe of a combat boot in my ribs. I turned my head sideways and looked up. There, standing tall, was Sergeant Major Basil Plumley. Plumley leaned down and shouted over the noise of the guns: 'You can't take no pictures laying down there on the ground, sonny.' . . . I thought: 'He's right. We're all going to die anyway, so I might as well take mine standing up.' I got up and began taking a few photographs." Galloway survived that action and went on to become a highly respected reporter of the Vietnam War.

Opposite: A wire-service photographer in a rice paddy in the Mekong Delta.

Khe Sanh was a U.S. Marine Corps base and airstrip located close to the Laos–South Vietnam border, south of the DMZ. Its location allowed troops to gather intelligence on traffic on the Ho Chi Minh Trail just inside the Laotian border, and to be a threat to operations in the immediate area. At the same time, its remote position made it difficult to reinforce or resupply if it were attacked and surrounded by a determined enemy.

On January 20, 1968, a marine reconnaissance patrol made contact with North Vietnamese Army (NVA) troops. The resulting skirmish was the first battle in what would become the siege of Khe Sanh.

Approximately thirty thousand NVA troops surrounded the six thousand marines stationed in Khe Sanh and its defensive outposts. For the next two months, the NVA launched a series of vicious attacks against the Americans. Unless the marines could be resupplied by air, they would be forced to surrender. Although the sieges were similar, Gen. Westmoreland vowed Khe Sanh would not be another Dien Bien Phu. He told his men, "We are not, repeat not, going to be defeated at Khe Sanh. I will tolerate no talking or even thinking to the contrary."

Operation Niagara, the aerial resupply of the marines at Khe Sanh, was launched. Despite bad weather and heavy antiaircraft defenses by the NVA, Operation Niagara kept the marines supplied. The aerial support became critical when an NVA rocket and artillery attack on January 21 hit the marines' main ammunition dump, destroying it. The ring of NVA antiaircraft batteries surrounding the marine base was like a noose. The air force transports flying supplies to the marines were under such constant enemy fire that they could no longer land on the airstrip. The only way they could discharge their cargo was in low-flying parachute drops.

Captain William H. Dabney commanded an outpost at Khe Sanh during the siege. Under constant attack from the enemy, he realized, "We needed something to jack up morale." What he and his men decided was that

Above: President Johnson (*second from left*) studies a model of the Khe Sanh area with his advisors.

Opposite: White phosphorous bomblets burning in midair create a smokescreen near the runway at Khe Sanh, prior to an airlift delivery of supplies and reinforcements.

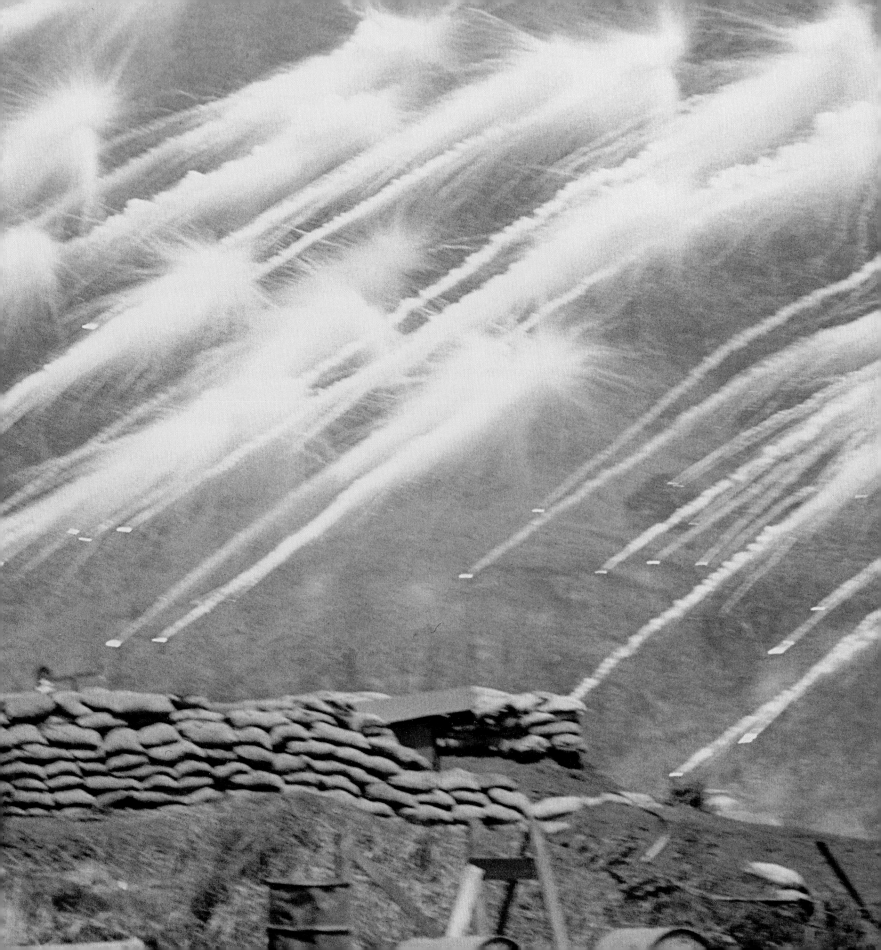

they'd raise the American flag—as an act of defiance against the enemy. He recalled, "So, daily at eight o'clock, precisely at eight o'clock, [the enemy] targeted us [with mortar and artillery fire], and we would raise the flag. We had good, deep holes right beside the flagpole, and it took about twenty-five seconds [to raise the flag] because we knew the time of flight for the [artillery] round was about twenty-five seconds. . . . We had a bugler, a lieutenant by the name of Matthews, who could do a fair rendition of the colors, albeit with speed. . . . The bugle had a way of getting shrapnel in it. It didn't sound right but it didn't matter. . . . It was a gesture of defiance. . . ."

Above: Marines riding on a M-48 tank.

Finally on April 1, 1968 the siege of Khe Sanh was successfully lifted. The defeated NVA retreated to their bases in Laos, having suffered an estimated ten thousand to fifteen thousand casualties. The marines suffered two thousand casualties. Marine historian Jack Shulimson observed, "Controversy still surrounds the battle. It is not known if the North Vietnamese really intended to take Khe Sanh or if the attack was merely a feint to lure U.S. forces away from the cities."

Gen. Giap claimed the battle was a victory for his forces, that the whole purpose of the attack was a diversion. If that was truly the case, then it was a costly diversion, because the marines estimated that two North Vietnamese Army divisions were destroyed during the siege.

Opposite: U.S. Army soldiers on their way to help relieve marines trapped at Khe Sanh.

QUICK FACTS

- U.S. Army soldier Gerry Schooler recalled a painful discovery during the Tet Offensive when he and another soldier were ordered to search for Viet Cong in a row of ruined homes. In one house, "in the very back, under this table, we found these 2 kids, obviously brother and sister, about 5, embraced, no doubt because they were so frightened. They were dead."

- Approximately 4,000 Viet Cong troops attacked targets in Saigon. Nineteen men, specially trained in the use of explosives, were assigned to attack the U.S. embassy.

- Construction was finished on the U.S. embassy compound only 3 months before the attack. The cost was $2.6 million, and the embassy was regarded as an impregnable fortress.

- For reasons that have never been explained, one group of targets the Communists did not attack during the first night of the Tet campaign were the private, off-base and lightly-guarded homes of top American military and political leaders. This allowed MACV to quickly coordinate a counterattack.

et—Vietnamese for "festival"—is the Vietnamese lunar new year and the most important holiday on the Vietnamese calendar. Because of its importance a cease-fire truce was observed during the three-day holiday so that both sides could celebrate in peace. And despite isolated instances of violence, such truces generally held. But in 1968, the Year of the Monkey, Gen. Giap planned a major surprise offensive to take advantage of the Tet holiday stand-down. Simultaneous attacks by the North Vietnamese Army and Viet Cong guerillas would be made at major cities and military bases throughout South Vietnam. Giap believed that this "general offensive" would inspire an uprising of the South Vietnamese populace, who would rally to the Communist cause and overthrow the government in Saigon.

On January 30, 1968, the Tet holiday began. Just after midnight the first attack was launched. Khe Sanh was surrounded. The ancient capital of Hue was overrun. In Saigon the Viet Cong staged attacks throughout the city. The most famous attack was on the American embassy, where a few Viet Cong managed to breach the outer wall and enter the compound, where they were quickly killed.

The Americans had received some warning of an impending attack, and thus were not completely taken by surprise. As the battle progressed, a major in the U.S. Fifth Cavalry jubilantly stated, "Here we've been waiting years for Charlie to surface and fight, and now he's doing just that—and getting his clock cleaned! Good chance he'll never recover from it. Stacking up to be a great tactical error on his part." Militarily the major was right. When it ended in March 1968, the Tet Offensive was a disaster for North Vietnam. Militarily it achieved none of its objectives. All the cities and villages attacked remained in American and South Vietnamese hands. Instead of joining the Communists, the populace rallied to the South Vietnamese government's side. The Communists suffered with more than fifty-eight thousand soldiers killed in the offensive, compared to fewer than four thousand U.S. troops and fewer than five thousand South Vietnamese troops killed. The Viet Cong were virtually wiped out, and from that point on were never an effective fighting force. The war would continue, but this time the North Vietnamese Army engaged in most of the battles.

Opposite: Civilians from Hue flee to safety.

But politically, it was an enormous strategic triumph for North Vietnam. The American news media reported the Tet Offensive as an American and South Vietnamese disaster. Part of the reason for this was that in the previous month, Gen. Westmoreland had made confident assurances that the war was almost won. Therefore the attack took the American public by surprise and gave the impression that the military leaders were wrong. Images of the dead Viet Cong inside the walled courtyard of the U.S. embassy caused many to question how a "weak" enemy could still be strong enough to blow a hole in the protective wall and attack the U.S. embassy.

The impression of a strong and implacable enemy was reinforced by the oftentimes biased news reports. With approximately five hundred accredited correspondents from one hundred and thirty news organizations in South Vietnam, the competition to be the first with a breaking story was intense. This was especially true of television reporters. Scenes of confused, even frightened, U.S. troops reacting to ambushes and sudden skirmishes were readily available. The result was a flood of lopsided reports that focused on the immediate and sensational events, devoid of analyses that could place the images into context. Howard K. Smith, a journalist for *ABC News*, said of the network's coverage, "Viet Cong casualties were one hundred times ours. But we never told the public that. We just showed pictures day after day of Americans getting [badly beaten]." General Maxwell Taylor later wrote, "In forming the popular concept of what had happened during the Tet offensive, TV was the dominant factor. The picture of a few flaming Saigon houses, presented by a gloomy-voiced telecaster . . . created the inevitable impression that this was the way it was in all or most of Saigon."

Military historian Brigadier General S. L. A. Marshall observed that "a potential major victory turned into a disastrous defeat through mistaken estimates, loss of nerve, and a tidal wave of defeatism." Due to a combination of Westmoreland's overoptimistic report, the administration's inability to unite the nation, and the majority of the American public desiring the war to end, President Johnson found himself in the same position the French were with Communist Vietnamese in 1954: He had to negotiate for peace with a resolute enemy.

Above: A street in the Saigon suburb of Cholon after the Tet Offensive.

Opposite: Saigon fire trucks race to buildings set afire by the Viet Cong during the Tet Offensive.

QUICK FACTS

- When 1968 ended, 536,100 U.S. military personnel were officially listed in Vietnam. This would be the peak strength of the U.S. military presence.

- Eight people were charged as the leaders of the violent protest at the Democratic National Convention: David Dellinger, Rennie Davis, Thomas Hayden, Abbie Hoffman, Jerry Rubin, Lee Weiner, John Froines, and Bobby Seale. Their trial on the charges of criminal responsibility with intent to riot became a raucous protest against the Vietnam War. The defendants were so disruptive that they were charged with 175 counts of contempt of court, and Seale was tried separately. The jury found all but Froines and Weiner guilty of inciting to riot. Their convictions were reversed in 1972.

- Chicago was the scene of more protests in 1969, when a radical organization called the Weathermen engaged in a series of violent demonstrations that became known as the "Days of Rage." The Weathermen had a Marxist philosophy and believed in a militant struggle against state and federal institutions. They carried out a terrorist campaign for several years bombing federal buildings. Federal law enforcement agencies cracked down on the organization, which had more than 600 members, and the organization no longer existed by the mid-1970s.

Above: Robert Kennedy was a senator from New York when he announced his intention to run for president on an antiwar platform.

President Johnson never went on campaign to fully explain to the American people why he was sending troops to Vietnam. He feared that if he did, it would destroy his program for domestic social and civil rights reform, titled the "Great Society." As he later said, "History provided too many cases where the sound of the bugle put an immediate end to the hopes and dreams of the best reformers. . . . Once the war began, then all those conservatives in the Congress would use it as a weapon against the Great Society. " Unfortunately, by not taking the initiative to gain the public's support through speeches that explained what was happening in Vietnam, President Johnson allowed those unhappy with the war to freely challenge his policies.

Disillusionment with the war in Vietnam mounted rapidly in late 1967. In September the newspaper *The Christian Science Monitor* reported that it had interviewed 205 members of Congress and 43 of them stated that they no longer supported the president's policy in Vietnam. The *New York Times* conducted its own survey of Congress in October and confirmed that congressional support was falling. And American people began to increasingly question the reasons why America was in Vietnam.

The Vietnam War would become the number one political topic for debate between Republicans and Democrats during the 1968 presidential election. Richard M. Nixon became the Republican candidate for the presidency. President Johnson had chosen not to seek reelection, and Vice President Humphrey had declared his candidacy. Under other circumstances, Humphrey would have been considered the favorite to succeed Johnson. But because the Vietnam War had become such a divisive issue, the Democratic field was wide open.

Early in the race Minnesota Senator Eugene McCarthy, a Democrat, openly announced a peace platform and succeeded in gaining the support of many antiwar activists. Another Democrat and presidential hopeful, Robert Kennedy, brother of former president John F. Kennedy, also announced a peace platform and received widespread support.

But the Vietnam War was not the only social issue dividing American society. President Johnson's Great Society's domestic reform program was an attempt to correct many social inequities that still existed in the country.

Opposite: Richard M. Nixon during the reception for the GOP presidential candidate, with his wife, Pat, beside him.

Above: With Dr. Martin Luther King Jr. and other civil rights leaders standing by, President Johnson signs the Civil Rights Bill in 1964.

Among the hallmarks of this program was the Voting Rights Act of 1965, which guaranteed African Americans the right to vote; the creation of Medicare, which provided medical assistance to the elderly; and the Elementary and Secondary Education Act, which granted federal aid to impoverished children. But the high cost of the war and the added cost of these social programs caused inflation to hurt the nation's economy. People saw the value of their money shrink, and some lost their jobs.

Also, the civil rights movement had become a major force in the country. Reports of racial tension and riots aroused emotions as bitter and violent as those about the Vietnam War. One of the most important civil rights leaders was Dr. Martin Luther King Jr. Originally King openly supported Johnson because of his Great Society agenda. But he grew concerned over the affect the Vietnam War might have on the recent civil rights and social gains. King's disillusionment grew when he read reports that showed that a larger-than-average number of men drafted were African American and that initially African-American troops suffered a larger share of battle casualties. King became the foremost antiwar advocate in the civil rights movement. And he vowed to make civil rights and the end of the Vietnam War major issues in the presidential election. A charismatic orator and leader, King gathered a rapidly-increasing following. He also became the target of racial hatred. On April 4, 1968 Dr. Martin Luther King Jr. was assassinated in Memphis, Tennessee.

The presidential campaign also became a bloody battleground. On June 5, Robert Kennedy was assassinated in California. And at the Democratic National Convention in Chicago, people watching television-news broadcasts were shocked to see Chicago police, Illinois state troopers, and National Guardsmen violently clash with thousands of antiwar demonstrators.

In November Americans went to the polls to vote. Hubert Humphrey, the Democratic candidate, was defeated by Richard Nixon. Nixon now had the responsibility of finding a way to get the United States out of Vietnam with as little controversy as possible. As events would prove, it would become an impossible goal.

Opposite: A confrontation between a demonstrator and National Guardsmen in Chicago during the Democratic National Convention.

QUICK FACTS

- The U.S. Army charged 14 men for crimes in the My Lai massacre. Lt. Calley was the only man convicted, receiving a sentence of life imprisonment. President Richard Nixon paroled Calley in November 1974.

- My Lai and the surrounding hamlets were nicknamed "Pinkville" because they contained Communist sympathizers—"pinkos." "Reds," a nickname for Communists because of the Red Communist flags, were members of the Communist Party, Viet Cong, or North Vietnamese Army troops.

- Approximately 100 students who had taken refuge in the Phu Cam Cathedral in Hue during the fighting were found and taken away by the Viet Cong. Their bodies, along with those of more than 300 others, were later found in a creek bed about 10 miles from Hue.

Atrocities, such as torturing or killing of unarmed, nonresisting civilians or prisoners, have been a part of war ever since war began. The most famous international agreements designed to punish those committing atrocities and to spell out rules of warfare on humanitarian issues are the ones established at the Geneva Convention. Additionally, each nation has its own laws. During the Vietnam War, both sides committed atrocities. American atrocities were spontaneous and random acts in direct violation of U.S. military law and MACV directives. In contrast, North Vietnam and the Viet Cong had a written policy that sanctioned and encouraged these acts, including assassination, massacre, and torture. Such acts came to symbolize the brutality of the Vietnam War: the massacre at My Lai, conducted by American troops, and the massacre in the South Vietnamese city of Hue during the Tet Offensive, conducted by Communist forces.

My Lai was a South Vietnamese hamlet. On March 16, 1968, Lieutenant William Calley Jr. led his platoon into My Lai as part of a search-and-destroy sweep to capture or kill suspected Viet Cong. Though the soldiers found only old men, women, and children, Calley, believing them to be Viet Cong, or Viet Cong sympathizers, ordered his men to attack. Calley was court-martialed for his actions. During his trial it was revealed that as many as five hundred civilians were massacred in what was later called by historians the most shameful act in U.S. Army history.

Hue was the historic cultural and intellectual center of Vietnam. When the Tet Offensive was launched, the Communists managed to seize most of the city. The monthlong battle to retake Hue would become the longest and bloodiest struggle during that campaign. During the fight against American and South Vietnamese forces, the Viet Cong swept through the city, conducting a systematic slaughter of intellectuals, doctors, political leaders, and anyone they judged "a cruel tyrant or reactionary element."

It was only after the Americans and South Vietnamese forces had recaptured Hue that they discovered what had occurred to the civilian population. During the postbattle cleanup and reconstruction of the city, they discovered mass graves of those slaughtered and executed. Searchers found 2,810 bodies, and additional records estimated that as many as 5,700 people—including foreign nationals—may have been killed by the Viet Cong.

Above: Lt. William Calley is escorted to the Fort Benning stockade to begin his life term in prison for his part in the My Lai massacre.

Opposite: A young widow holding the photograph of her husband slain by Communist forces at Hue.

"WE GOTTA GET OUTTA THIS PLACE"— MUSIC OF THE VIETNAM WAR

Rock 'n' roll music was an important part of the American troops' lives in Vietnam. It was a reminder of home in an otherwise foreign and dangerous place. The major broadcast source for music was the Armed Forces Radio, which taped Top 40 songs in recording studios in Los Angeles and had them airlifted to Vietnam. The military had a number of restrictions about the type of music that could be played. Protest songs, and any music that could be interpreted as a protest, were prohibited. One of the most notable top hits in 1966 on the approved playlist was "The Ballad of the Green Berets," a patriotic song written and performed by Staff Sergeant Barry Sadler.

Enlisted men became bored with the approved playlists for the Armed Forces Radio stations because they were dominated by classical music or light pop tunes. As a result soldiers began bringing their own music to play on their stereos. One of the most popular songs among the enlisted men was "We Gotta Get Outta This Place" by the Animals.

Professional musicians had a big impact on the antiwar movement. Folk singers Bob Dylan, Joan Baez, and Pete Seeger composed songs and performed in antiwar concerts. The most famous rock concert during the Vietnam War period was Woodstock, held in upstate New York in 1968. The theme song of the concert, "Woodstock," performed by Crosby, Stills, Nash, and Young, had an antiwar theme. Jimi Hendrix, who had served in Vietnam in the 101st Airborne, was the dominant performer of a new style of psychedelic music called "acid rock" that utilized the electric guitar in ways never before imagined. One of his most popular songs was "Purple Haze," which had references to the purple smoke used to mark landing zones for helicopters. Though his music and the hard-edged rebellious music of Janis Joplin, Jefferson Airplane, and similar groups did not break the Top-10 charts, they had widespread air time both in the United States and in South Vietnam. In 1970 the antiwar movement had as an anthem a powerful antiwar song by Edwin Starr that was simply titled, "War."

It was this element of protest that separated the music of the Vietnam War from music in all earlier American wars. Previously, the music was patriotic or supportive: An antiwar song was an exception. In the Vietnam War, an antiwar song was more the rule.

Opposite: A marine carrying his M-16 and guitar at Khe Sanh.

QUICK FACTS

- In a speech on November 3, 1969, President Nixon first used the phrase "silent majority" to refer to unpublicized supporters of his policies, in contrast to protestors who received much media attention. The speech said in part, "If a vocal minority prevails over reason and the will of the majority, this nation has no future as a free society. . . . And so tonight—you, the great silent majority of my fellow Americans—I ask for your support."

- A major event in the antiwar movement occurred in November 1969, when an estimated 500,000 participants staged a protest march in Washington, D.C.

- On May 4, 1970, at Kent State University in Ohio, a student antiwar protest ended tragically when Ohio National Guardsmen fired on student protestors, killing 4 and wounding 9. This event became the subject of the hit song "Ohio," by Crosby, Stills, Nash, and Young.

Above: Antiwar protestors demonstrating in Wichita, Kansas.

Originally in the early 1960s most people accepted the government's claim that U.S. troops were in South Vietnam to stop the spread of Communism. But as the years passed, America did not seem to be gaining ground even though an increasing number of troops were sent to South Vietnam. By 1968 many people from all walks of life began to question why the United States was involved.

Those opposing the war ran the gamut from Students for a Democratic Society (SDS), to far-right conservative groups, to nonpartisan organizations, to civil rights groups. Their motives were equally diverse. College students subject to military service became draft resisters. Religious groups, such as the Quakers, protested for religious reasons. Some civil-rights groups saw the money spent on the war as being taken from money needed to fight the war on poverty and inequality. Civil rights leader Dr. Martin Luther King Jr., who had won the Nobel Peace Prize in 1964, said in a speech in 1967, "[W]e have been repeatedly faced with the cruel irony of watching Negro and white boys on TV screens as they kill and die together for a nation that has been unable to seat them together in the same schools."

In 1965 a poll showed more than half of Americans supported the war. In 1967 polls showed that only thirty-five percent of the American people supported it. Responding to this shift, senators and members of Congress who supported President Johnson began speaking out, questioning the strategic necessity of the war.

But the true shift in sentiment was due to the fact that President Johnson had never fully communicated to the American people why it was important to be in South Vietnam. This failure, coupled with the lack of perceived success and the growing number of dead soldiers, caused more and more people of all ages and backgrounds to raise their voices against the war. This antiwar movement would come to include the nonpartisan organization Vietnam Veterans Against the War. Though never gathered into one overall group and having different motivations, these protestors— students and blue-collar workers, veterans and businesspeople—were united in their desire to end the war.

When Richard Nixon was elected president in 1968, his priority was to find a way to get the United States out of South Vietnam.

Opposite: Veterans marching in Washington, D.C., demanding that the troops in Vietnam be brought home.

QUICK FACTS

• The Selective Service System was composed of almost 4,000 local draft boards and staffed by unpaid volunteers, most of whom were white males who were veterans of earlier wars. A 1966 survey of 16,638 board members of the draft revealed that only 1.3 percent were African American. Women were not allowed to serve on draft boards until 1967.

• Women were not affected by the draft. All women who served in the military were volunteers.

• One favorite option for white upper-middle-class males wishing to serve in the military but avoid the possibility of being stationed in Vietnam was to join the National Guard. In 1968 only 1 percent of the Army National Guard troops were African American.

• More than 57 percent of the eligible males from 1964 to 1973 received deferments. Only 2 percent, or approximately 520,000 young men, committed draft violations.

Above: The front and back of a Selective Service registration card, also known as the draft card.

During the Vietnam War, men were inducted into the military services in one of two ways: they either volunteered or they were conscripted by law. Conscription into the military under the Selective Service System—the "draft"—affected approximately twenty-six million American males ages eighteen to twenty-four during the Vietnam War. The purpose of the draft was to provide a sufficient source of manpower to fill the ranks of the different services. The intent was that all men, excepting those with medical disabilities, should be obligated for service. But the reality fell short. The draft was unfairly administered, filled with loopholes that allowed a young man to avoid military service through deferments. The most abused of these were the college deferments, which favored the affluent and well-educated American males of draft age.

James Lafferty, an activist lawyer who established a number of draft counseling centers in the midwest, advised young men about the legal means available to them to avoid the draft. He observed, "Every aspect of the draft had a built-in bias against the poorest young men in the country." One deferment that, on the surface, appeared to favor the poor was the "hardship" deferment. But as Lafferty pointed out, "If you were an unemployed kid in inner-city Detroit and your mom was on welfare, military service might actually improve your economic circumstances and give you more money to send home to your mom, while the wealthy could claim that military service would be an economic crisis if the circumstances were right."

The men most passionately opposed to the war chose to emigrate rather than be drafted. Canada, because of its shared border with the United States and its similar culture, was the country most often used for this. Tim O'Brien, who graduated from college in 1968, was drafted and shipped to Vietnam in 1969. He later observed, "There were a lot of us in Vietnam who didn't want to be there, and many of us didn't have the courage to do what the resisters did. It took a lot of courage to cross the border and leave behind your family and your hometown and your girlfriend. . . . I ended up going to Vietnam just to protect my reputation and sense of self-esteem, but the guys who went to Canada somehow were able to find the moral courage to make a choice they knew was gonna dog them the rest of their lives."

Opposite: A student burns what he claims is his draft card.

QUICK FACTS

- Numerous attempts were made to rescue American POWs. The operations were given the umbrella name of Code Name Bright Light. None of the rescue operations were successful. Reasons for the failure included faulty intelligence, POWs being moved just before the mission, or delays in launching the rescue mission.

- American POWs were kept in a number of prisons, some of which were nicknamed: Briar-patch, Faith, Hope (the nickname for Son Tay), Skidrow, D-1, Rockpile, Plantation, the Zoo, Alcatraz, and Dogpatch.

- Estimates of POW deaths in captivity vary. The North Vietnamese officially listed 55 deaths. U.S. sources range from 54 to 72.

- The longest-held POW was Army Special Forces Captain Floyd James Thompson, who was captured on March 26, 1964. He was released on March 16, 1973.

Above: The receipt for Captain Robert White, officially regarded as the last American prisoner of war released after the Vietnam War.

President Johnson's decision to not ask Congress to declare war against North Vietnam in the wake of the Tonkin Gulf incident in 1964, when North Vietnamese patrol boats attacked U.S. Navy destroyers, would have tragic consequences for American servicemen captured by the Viet Cong and North Vietnamese. Under the Geneva Convention, which contains rules of conduct during war, combatants captured by the enemy are designated prisoners of war—POWs—and rules regarding their treatment are clearly spelled out.

But the North Vietnamese government exploited the legal fact that a declared state of war did not exist between the United States and North Vietnam. The North Vietnamese government claimed that captured U.S. military personnel were *not* POWs; instead, they stated, these prisoners were criminals, and thus did not fall under the protection of the Geneva Conventions.

As a result, captured Americans found themselves subject to torture and other atrocities. American POWs were kept in a number of prisons. The most famous of them was Hoa Lo, known by its more famous nickname the "Hanoi Hilton," located in North Vietnam's capital.

Colonel Lawrence R. Bailey was a POW captured in Laos while on a secret mission. When he was captured, he weighed 185 pounds. When he was released, his weight was 115 pounds. His captivity included long stretches in solitary confinement. He recalled, "Small things began to take on major significance. A nail in the wall and a pinhole in the tin [sheet] covering the window became two of the most important [things] in my seventeen months of solitary confinement." The nail was used as a tool to mark the days, allowing him to keep a calendar and to enlarge the hole in the tin sheet. Once he had made it large enough, he could, by standing on tiptoe, look out onto the street. He later said, "That peephole enabled me through my imagination to leave the cell for hours at a time each day and participate in the lives" of people who walked past his prison.

The POWs were officially released in a ceremony following the signing of the Paris Peace Accords in January 27, 1973. The POWs had a wide range of reactions when they received news of their release. One POW, Sam Johnson, recalled that men in his group "ran to each other, hugging and crying and whooping with joy."

Opposite: A wounded barefoot air force officer, captured by Communist forces, being escorted through a city in North Vietnam.

QUICK FACTS

- During the war, national television-news broadcasts would include daily body count statistics in their reports on the Vietnam War.

- Local tribespeople called Ap Bia Mountain "the mountain of the crouching beast."

- One of the most famous quotes about the fighting in the Vietnam War came from a nameless soldier's letter home, written during the fighting on Hamburger Hill. The quote, at the end of the letter, read, "You may not be able to read this. I am writing this in a hurry. I see death coming up the hill."

- Armies throughout history have experienced isolated incidences of violence against superior officers by enlisted troops. In the Vietnam War these acts in American units were called "fragging incidents." Fragging was the use of fragmentation grenades by enlisted military personnel to murder fellow soldiers—usually officers or sergeants judged to be incompetent, and thus dangerous to troops in combat. Though the actual incidents were very few, they became more common in 1969 when units experienced discipline problems and a decline of qualified leaders as a result of the rapid turnover of troops due to the one-year tour-of-duty rule.

For months after the Tet Offensive, ground combat between North Vietnamese Army troops and American and South Vietnamese forces had declined significantly. The major reason for this was that North Vietnam had to recoup the losses it had suffered during the Tet Offensive and train new recruits. One of the areas it needed to rebuild was its base in the A Shau Valley. The A Shau Valley is located in the northwestern part of South Vietnam, not far from the DMZ and on the border with Laos. It had long been a major base for the North Vietnamese Army. During the monsoon season of early 1969, the Communists began stockpiling huge stores of weapons, ammunition, and supplies. They were also constructing new buildings and bunkers that would make the camp an impregnable staging area for future offensives.

To disrupt this construction and destroy North Vietnamese units in this sanctuary, MACV planned a campaign code-named "Operation Apache Snow." Launched on May 10, 1969 it was a combined forces assault that included U.S. Army and Marines, and South Vietnamese Army troops as well as air strikes.

On the second day of the operation, American troops seized Dong Ap Bia—Ap Bia Mountain. Normally Communist forces would have retreated into the jungle. But this time they chose to stay and fight. What happened next was a battle so severe and bloody that troops called it a "meat grinder."

The fighting raged from May 11 to May 20, 1969. When it was over, the enemy was severely mauled, having suffered an estimated 630 dead. U.S. troops suffered fifty-six men killed, and the South Vietnamese Army lost five men. After the fighting was over and the U.S. troops were clearing up the battlefield, one soldier nailed onto a tree a cardboard sign that read, HAMBURGER HILL. A short time later another soldier added the words, "Was it worth it?"

Because the purpose of the campaign was to kill enemy troops and not to seize and occupy territory, when Operation Apache Snow ended on June 7, 1969, the American and South Vietnamese troops returned to their bases. Shortly after they left, Communists reoccupied the area. This caused a huge uproar in the United States. The fight on Hamburger Hill seemed to symbolize the futility of winning battles in Vietnam without achieving a victory.

Opposite: A wounded U.S. paratrooper awaiting a dustoff at a base camp near Hamburger Hill.

On May 20, on the floor of the Senate, Massachusetts Senator Edward M. Kennedy denounced the attack on Dong Ap Bia, calling it "senseless and irresponsible . . . madness . . . American boys are too valuable to be sacrificed for a false sense of military pride." General Creighton Abrams defended the battle, stating, "We are not fighting for terrain as such. We are going after the enemy." And Texas Senator John Tower added that with regard to reaching a peace settlement, "Unless we are prepared to surrender to the enemy, we must negotiate from a position of strength."

But such thoughts of strategy and peace were part of a different world from the one where the troops in Vietnam lived. Patrick Power, a nineteen-year-old soldier who fought on Hamburger Hill, later wrote, "I didn't know anyone who was not frightened. It's just a matter of being nineteen or twenty years old and being scared, not knowing, not having any control as to what's happening. . . . At the end of the battle, we had to identify the bodies, or what there was left of them, [and] bag them up for the next day. . . . I was just glad I was out, and I think everyone was very elated that they were alive."

Above: A soldier stares down into the fog-shrouded A Shau Valley.

Opposite: A soldier gathers up barbed wire surrounding a camp in the A Shau Valley.

QUICK FACTS

- Reconnaissance teams were called "spike teams" and had the call sign "ST." Their purpose on a mission was to observe the enemy and avoid contact as much as possible. Combat teams assigned to initiate contact with the enemy were called "hatchet teams" and had the call sign "HT."

- U.S. bombings of North Vietnamese and Viet Cong positions in Laos totaled almost 2.1 million tons, more than the amount dropped by the United States in Europe and the Pacific during World War II.

- The CIA used airplanes and crews to conduct secret intelligence operations in Laos. The cover name for the group was "Air America."

- The U.S. teams often worked with members of the indigenous tribes, Huk and Montagnards, who hated the Vietnamese. Many of the special-operations men formed very close bonds with the tribespeople.

Above: President Nixon during a press conference on Vietnam and Cambodia.

The countries of Laos and Cambodia form the western borders of North and South Vietnam. During the Vietnam War both small nations were neutral. But their land still became a battleground in the Vietnam War. The U.S. government knew that North Vietnam and the Viet Cong were violating that neutrality with base camps, supply depots, rest centers, and the Ho Chi Minh Trail supply route constructed within their borders. Because Laos and Cambodia were militarily weak countries, they could do nothing to stop Communists' violation of their territory. In contrast the United States officially honored the neutrality and ordered its forces not to pursue the enemy across those borders. This official policy infuriated many people in America, who thought Communists had no right to refuge.

But what the people did not know was that under President Johnson's leadership, the government had an unofficial policy—a covert program—for fighting Communist forces in Laos and Cambodia. Later, after the facts about it were revealed to the general public by the press, the campaign was known as "the Secret War." This program used a variety of special-force units, including the Green Berets, SEALs, Air Commandos, and Force Recon, as well as the CIA.

These units would infiltrate known enemy sites and attack installations, sabotage the Ho Chi Minh Trail, monitor troop movements, and call in airstrikes, as well as conduct intelligence-gathering missions. The units even set up their own observation sites and camps.

When Richard Nixon became president, he upped the stakes in the Secret War in order to force Communists to the bargaining table. In May 1970 a series of raids in Cambodia captured vast stores of North Vietnamese equipment and supplies, including 23,000 individual weapons, 2,500 mortars, machine guns and artillery pieces, 16.7 million rounds of small-arms ammunition, and 14 million pounds of rice. But the military success came too late. At this point the majority of Congress wanted the United States out of Vietnam, regardless of the consequences. In 1970 Congress passed a series of resolutions and legislative initiatives that limited the executive power of the president. The most important of these stopped the funding for any military action in the region beyond the borders of South Vietnam.

Opposite: Two South Vietnamese Special Forces soldiers push a cart through a burning hut as they carry out a scorched-earth operation against a Communist supply area along the Cambodian border.

On November 3, 1969 President Nixon, as part of his promise to withdraw U.S. forces from Vietnam, formally announced a program he called "Vietnamization." It would be an orderly transfer of all U.S. assets—military bases, arms, vehicles, aircraft, ammunition, and supplies—to the South Vietnamese Army and Navy after they had been trained in their use and upkeep. This was an ambitious program, and because of domestic antiwar sentiment, it had to happen fast.

In truth having the South Vietnamese fight their own war had been an American goal since the long-ago days of the military advisors. Subsequent military and political events had caused modifications of that intent, resulting in the United States shouldering most of the war-making burden. Even so, the advisor program had never been completely disbanded.

The tumultuous events of 1968 had caused most government leaders to demand the transition be made as quickly as possible. Though the Tet Offensive had caused the South Vietnamese to rally to their government and the South Vietnamese troops to fight for their nation, not all American mili-tary and political leaders in South Vietnam were convinced that the country could survive on its own. But regardless of their doubts, the political reality in the United States, with its strong antiwar sentiment, made Vietnamization a must-do program.

The pressure on the U.S. military leaders was enormous. On November 2, 1968, new MACV commander Gen. Creighton Abrams held a briefing on the transition. Abrams had just returned from Washington, D.C., where everyone was concerned about the imminent general election. Having just traveled more than seven thousand miles, he was tired. The first briefing officer was an air force colonel who pre-sented the air force's plan using an elaborate slide show to illustrate with various charts and graphs the transition process. His conclusion was that the turnover would take eight years and be successfully completed in 1976.

Gen. Abrams slammed his fist down on the table and shouted, "There is no longer a consensus of support for the

Above: South Vietnamese troops fire at North Vietnamese positions during fighting in the northern Mekong Delta in South Vietnam.

Opposite: Gen. Creighton Abrams, at the head of the table, in a luncheon meeting with presidential advisors.

war back in the United States. [1976 is] out of the question! . . . The president wants to get the war turned over as soon as possible. We have to make that happen."

President Nixon later recalled, "Our principal objectives shifted [from the military defeat of Communists] to protecting the South Vietnamese at

Above: Gen. Creighton Abrams, who succeeded Gen. Westmoreland as head of MACV.

the village level, reestablishing the local political process, and winning the loyalty of the peasants by involving them in the government and providing them with economic opportunity."

At the same time that Vietnamization was put into action, a schedule was created to return American combat troops to the United States. American advisors supervised the transition of now-abandoned American military bases and equipment to the South Vietnamese. Despite enormous difficulties, it did happen. The first problem faced by the advisors was the Vietnamese language itself. Because it is a language that evolved around agriculture and its needs, the technical vocabulary required for the weapons, transport, and mechanical equipment did not exist. Fortunately enough South Vietnamese soldiers knew some English, so all technical communication was done in English.

The gradual return of American units to the United States continued so that, by 1972, all but a small group of military advisors remained in South Vietnam. U.S. ambassador to South Vietnam Ellsworth Bunker observed, "Considering that the country was at war, I think it was quite remarkable how well the government functioned."

Opposite: A South Vietnamese regional-forces trooper in 1970.

With Vietnamization now the official U.S. policy, more and more responsibility for conducting the war in Vietnam was given to the South Vietnamese government. Operation Lam Son, a campaign to cut off supplies coming down the Ho Chi Minh Trail, was the first real test of the Vietnamization program. Though American war planes and helicopters would assist in the fighting, all the ground troops would be from the South Vietnamese Army.

Operation Lam Son was launched on February 8, 1971, when fifteen thousand South Vietnamese Army troops invaded Laos and rushed to sever the Ho Chi Minh Trail at a town named Tchépone, just twenty-five miles west of Khe Sanh. The South Vietnamese assault stalled after advancing twelve miles. The North Vietnamese fought back hard and rushed reinforcements into the threatened area. American air power was of little help at first because heavy fog prevented effective air attack. Later, when the weather cleared, the North Vietnamese forces were well prepared with deadly antiaircraft defenses that included cannon, heavy machine guns, and surface-to-air missiles.

On March 6, South Vietnamese troops captured the town of Tchépone. But the victory was short-lived. With more and more North Vietnamese troops arriving, the South Vietnamese units became outnumbered and were forced to retreat. They came under constant attack during the retreat and would have been slaughtered had it not been for American air support.

In a scenario typical of the Vietnam War experience, politicians in both North Vietnam and in the United States saw elements of success in the battle to support their program and strategy. On April 7, 1971 President Nixon, in a televised speech to the nation, announced, "Tonight I can report Vietnamization has succeeded." At the same time, the North Vietnam government declared that Operation Lam Son was "the heaviest defeat ever for Nixon and Company."

Above: South Vietnamese soldiers in an armored troop carrier.

NORTH VIETNAM

DMZ

17th Parallel

Quang Tri

Hue

Khe Sanh

LAOS

Da Nang

Hoi An

THAILAND

Mekong River

Military Region I

Quang Ngai

Kon Tum

Pleiku

Qui Nhon

SOUTH
VIETNAM

Song Cau

CAMBODIA

Mekong River

Ban Me Thuot

Military Region II

Nha Trang

Snuol

Chup

Gia Nghia

Da Lat

Phnom Penh

Bao Loc

Phan Rang

Tay Ninh

Bien
Hoa

Cao Lanh

Phan Thiet

Long Xuyen

My Tho

Ham Tan

Phuoc Tuy

*South
China
Sea*

Ben Tre

Saigon

Military Region III

Rach Gia

Can Tho

Khanh Hung

*Gulf of
Thailand*

Military Region IV

Quang Long

N
W E
S

U.S. Military Regions
of South Vietnam

0   50   100 miles

0   50   100 kilometers

In 1972 President Nixon's Vietnamization program had reduced the number of ground troops in South Vietnam from a peak strength of 536,100 to 65,000 men. The North Vietnamese government, well aware of this reduction, believed now was the time to strike a decisive blow in South Vietnam. Even with the American Air Force and Navy stationed nearby, they felt that it would be easy to defeat the South Vietnamese Army. Gen. Giap laid plans for the largest offensive in the war. The name he chose for his operation was the Nguyen Hue campaign, but because it was launched on the Easter holiday, Americans called it the "Easter Offensive."

On March 30, 1972 the North Vietnamese Army launched a massive multiprong attack through the Demilitarized Zone in the north, from sanctuaries in Cambodia, through the Central Highlands in the middle, and just above Saigon in the south. Communists were aided by bad weather that grounded all aircraft. Confusion and fear swept the South Vietnamese Army ranks. Resistance was spotty. Some units were overrun, others panicked, still others put up a spirited defense that delayed enemy advances.

Marine Lieutenant Colonel G. H. Turly, an American advisor during this period, later recounted one act of extraordinary heroism among the South Vietnamese, writing, "Sergeant Luom and his rocket team remained in their assigned position. . . . [T]he first T-54 tank arrived at the north end of the bridge. The classic confrontation between an Asian 'David' and a forty-ton steel 'Goliath' was about to begin. . . . The spectacle of this ninety-five-pound marine lying in the direct path of a forty-ton tank . . . was in one respect incredibly mad. In another more important respect, it was incredibly inspiring. . . ." Taking careful aim with his handheld antitank rocket launcher called a LAAW, Sgt. Luom fired, hitting the tank at a key spot, which temporarily stopped the North Vietnamese's main ground attack.

Initially the North Vietnamese had great success. But as the weather cleared, American warplanes were able to launch aerial counterattacks. Also, mines were laid in the important North Vietnam port of Haiphong, cutting off supplies. Though fighting continued into the summer, the South Vietnamese Army was able to launch a counteroffensive that drove the North Vietnamese out in June 1972. The failed Easter Offensive proved that President Nixon's Vietnamization policy seemed to be working.

Above: A South Vietnamese marine carries the body of his dead comrade.

Opposite: South Vietnamese medic and refugees dash for cover during a Communist attack on the South Vietnamese capital.

THE LINEBACKER OPERATIONS

QUICK FACTS

- One reason for Linebacker I's success was that President Nixon allowed his military advisors the freedom to decide which targets to attack and how often to attack them. President Johnson refused to do that in the Operation Rolling Thunder air campaign. Air force and navy commanders believed that President Johnson's refusal made it impossible to effectively bomb enemy targets.

- It took just 11 days of bombing to bring the North Vietnamese to the negotiating table. Many U.S. airmen believed that if President Johnson had allowed them to conduct a similar all-out campaign with Operation Rolling Thunder, the Vietnam War could have ended much earlier.

- There are an estimated 15 million large bomb craters in Vietnam. Most still exist, causing those areas to look pitted like the surface of the moon. The only difference is that the holes in Vietnam are filled with water and surrounded by plants.

Above: The aftermath of a B-52 air-strike mission on Vietnamese farmland leaves the countryside pockmarked with bomb craters, now filled with water.

While President Nixon's Vietnamization program had led to the evacuation of most American ground troops from South Vietnam, the U.S. government was still committed to the defense of its ally. It backed up that pledge of support with the use of air power in two campaigns known as Linebacker I and Linebacker II.

Linebacker I was launched on May 10, 1972 in response to North Vietnam's Easter Offensive in March. Using precision-guided munitions—the so-called "smart" bombs that contained small computerized aiming devices, unlike the previous bombs that had no "brain" and were simply dropped from planes—for the first time U.S. Air Force and Navy planes attacked highways, railroads, bridges, and warehouses as well as troop targets. When the operation ended, the bombings had severely disrupted the flow of supplies to the invading troops, causing the offensive to stall. Thanks to Linebacker I, the South Vietnamese Army was able to successfully counterattack and drive the invaders out.

Later that year, representatives from the United States, South Vietnam, North Vietnam, and the Viet Cong met in Paris, France, to discuss a peace treaty. The U.S. government became more and more frustrated because no progress was made in the meetings. The North Vietnamese representatives made unreasonable demands, including one that called for South Vietnam to disband its army while allowing North Vietnam to station its army in the south. And, after having made their demands, the North Vietnamese representatives would refuse to budge from their positions. Eventually, the talks broke off altogether. Finally, on December 13, 1972, President Nixon issued an ultimatum to the North Vietnamese government, demanding that it return to the negotiation table "or else." When it refused, the president authorized the resumption of the air attack over North Vietnam. Linebacker II was launched on December 18, 1972. Called the "Christmas Bombings" by the United States press, B-52 bombers and other planes attacked strategic targets and antiaircraft defenses in Hanoi and in North Vietnam's major port city, Haiphong, as well as other locations. On December 28, the North Vietnamese government agreed to reopen negotiations.

Opposite: B-52 *Stratofortress* dropping bombs.

The Paris peace talks were a series of attempts to reach a negotiated settlement to the Vietnam War. The first attempt was initiated by the United States in 1968, shortly after the conclusion of the Tet Offensive. President Johnson announced on March 31, 1968, that the United States would stop bombing targets in North Vietnam and negotiate a peaceful settlement. The North Vietnamese government agreed, and representatives from both sides arranged to meet in Paris to discuss how to end the war in Vietnam. Thus began long, torturous, and often futile negotiations that would continue off and on until 1973.

There were many points of contention. The two most significant were that the North Vietnamese government refused to recognize the legitimacy of the South Vietnamese government and that the South Vietnamese government refused to agree to allow the Viet Cong a voice in the negotiations. At times it seemed that neither side was serious about ending the war.

After Richard Nixon became president in 1969, he added a second—and secret—chain of talks with Communists. This series of talks was led by National Security Advisor Dr. Henry Kissinger. Secret negotiations occurring simultaneously with public ones regarding peace treaties are not unusual. Sometimes there are subjects so sensitive that if any news of their discussion were made public, it would wreck negotiations. The Vietnam War had many complex and volatile issues that had to be resolved. The most important included the guarantee of South Vietnamese sovereignty, the withdrawal of all Communist troops from South Vietnam, and the repatriation of all American POWs. It was these secret discussions, together with the failure of North Vietnam's Easter Offensive and the follow-up of the United States's Linebacker I and II bombing raids that finally broke the deadlock in the negotiations.

On January 27, 1973, the "Agreement on Ending the War and Restoring Peace in Vietnam" was signed in Paris by the United States, North Vietnam, South Vietnam, and the Viet Cong. The key clause was that all U.S. troops would leave South Vietnam within sixty days simultaneously with the return of all American POWs.

But before the ink was even dry on the treaty documents, both North and South Vietnam were violating the cease-fire truce. The only clause honored was the departure of all American troops and the eventual release of American POWs. Fighting would continue in Vietnam for two more years.

Above: Wives of marine POWs at Camp Pendleton, waiting for their freed husbands to emerge from the airplane that has brought them home.

Opposite: President Nixon (*right*) with his National Security Advisor, Dr. Kissinger (*left*).

Daniel Ellsberg worked for the government as an intelligence analyst for the Defense Department in the mid-1960s. He assisted in compiling the 1967 classified study of U.S. efforts in Vietnam. Every aspect of the war was studied in detail, beginning with the origins of the conflict in 1940 and ending with the escalating war. Ultimately the study totaled more than seven thousand pages.

Ellsberg found that the government had misled its citizens about a war many of its own experts felt could not be won. In 1969 he began copying parts of the study. His next step was very difficult. The publicizing of classified government documents is a serious offense. Because the papers he now had dealt with national security issues, Ellsberg could be tried for violating the Espionage Act. But Ellsberg felt that it was worth risking the threat of imprisonment to tell the full truth about the U.S. efforts in Vietnam.

In 1971 he gave his documents to the *New York Times*. The first of these documents, which came to be known as the "Pentagon Papers," were published on June 13, 1971. President Nixon was furious when he discovered what had happened. He tried to get the publication of these documents stopped, but the Supreme Court overruled him.

The White House authorized the use of illegal wiretaps of Ellsberg's phone and the burglary of his psychiatrist's office. Ellsberg was arrested and brought to trial, which was declared a mistrial. The second trial was dismissed by the judge when President Nixon's abuse of power regarding Ellsberg became public.

But Nixon's abuses of power extended far beyond Daniel Ellsberg. They also included illegal wiretaps of reporters' telephones, spying on White House staffers, and the attempted burglary of the offices of the Democratic National Committee in the Watergate Hotel by a specially trained team of men. Nixon wanted to obtain information about the Democratic presidential campaign plans.

The series of abuses of power and the following cover-up attempts came to be known as the "Watergate scandal," named after the hotel where police had captured the burglars. The scandal would result in a chain of hearings and trials that led to calls for impeachment of the president. Nixon avoided impeachment by resigning from office on August 9, 1974.

Above: Washington Post reporters Carl Bernstein (left) and Robert Woodward (right), who had reported the Watergate scandal.

Opposite: President Nixon gesturing toward transcripts of tape recordings of meetings during his administration in the White House.

QUICK FACTS

- Because of the chaos surrounding the last days of the war and the evacuation, no one knows the exact count of the number of orphans rescued. It is estimated that 14,000 orphans were successfully evacuated by air. The orphans were sent to a variety of countries, including the United States.

- In 1974 Hubert H. Humphrey, vice president under President Johnson, said of the Vietnam War, "We overestimated our ability to control events, which is one of the great dangers of a great power. Power tends to be a substitute for judgment and wisdom."

- After North Vietnam conquered South Vietnam and united the country, they changed the name of Saigon to Ho Chi Minh City, in honor of their leader, who had died in 1969.

Above: South Vietnamese orphans in an airplane flying them to the United States.

In 1975 the United States had only a small staff at its embassy and a few military advisors in Saigon. On January 8, 1975 the North Vietnamese government, in defiance of the peace treaty signed in Paris, launched a major offensive against South Vietnam. The attack revealed that North Vietnam had never lost its desire to conquer South Vietnam. Without the backup of U.S. air power, weaknesses in the South Vietnamese Army were exposed: too many officers were corrupt or incompetent; supplies were inadequate; and maintenance of vehicles was often inconsistent. And, above all, South Vietnam did not have a strong central government that could rally and inspire its people. One after another, major cities fell.

Panic engulfed South Vietnamese citizens. Many feared they would be imprisoned or executed by the North Vietnamese. As conditions worsened, the U.S. government started evacuating people. The first was Operation Babylift, begun on April 2, 1975, the evacuation of South Vietnamese orphans. U.S. Army General Homer Smith, who was responsible, recalled that April 4, 1975, was "probably the longest day of my life." That day a transport plane carrying two hundred and twenty-six South Vietnamese orphans and seventy-seven Americans crash-landed shortly after takeoff as a result of engine failure. One hundred and thirty-three orphans, thirty-three civilians, and eleven crew members died in the crash. "It was a shattering, shattering experience," Gen. Smith recalled.

On April 29 Operation Frequent Wind, the final evacuation of U.S. personnel and select South Vietnamese citizens, was initiated. The conditions were chaotic. Marine Sergeant Russell Thurman was stationed aboard the USS *Okinawa*, which was one of the primary refugee recovery ships. "The sky was filled with helicopters, and most of them weren't ours," he recalled. So many unauthorized helicopters were landing on ships that crew members were forced to shove the empty Vietnamese helicopters overboard.

For many Americans, the most vivid image is of people climbing the roof of the American embassy to embark onto an awaiting Huey helicopter. For others it was the image of North Vietnamese tanks crashing through the gates of the presidential palace. For everyone, though, one fact stood out: After all the broken diplomatic promises and agreements, with the North Vietnamese Army in complete possession of South Vietnam on April 30, 1975, the war in Vietnam was finally over.

Opposite: South Vietnamese citizens swarming over the wall of the U.S. embassy in Saigon.

Of the many contentious issues left unsettled at the conclusion of the Vietnam War, the most traumatic and emotional was the fate of American servicemen officially labeled "missing in action"—the MIAs. Even the number of MIAs at the end of the war—twenty-five hundred—is in dispute. One of the agreements in the 1973 Paris Peace Accords provided for the return of all U.S. POWs and assistance regarding MIAs.

The political debate on whether North Vietnam—later Vietnam—had returned all American prisoners or were secretly keeping some was a recurrent political flashpoint. In 1979, under pressure from the National League of Families of American Prisoners and Missing in Southeast Asia and other organizations, Congress officially changed the classification of status of soldiers listed as "killed in action" (KIA) but whose remains had not been recovered back to POW/MIA. This allowed family members to receive higher government benefits as well as restoring the hope that missing troops might still be alive. President Reagan in 1982 stated that he believed some Americans were still being held against their will in Southeast Asia, and directed that the POW/MIA flag be flown over the White House one day per year. By 1990 all fifty states had an official National POW/MIA Recognition Day. The subject of MIAs was also a topic in the U.S. presidential election in 1992. Presidential candidate Ross Perot stated that he believed there were some Americans still being held prisoner.

In 1992 an international Joint Task Force-Full Accounting (JTF-FA) was created to determine the fate of the MIAs. The JTF-FA organizes teams of searchers in cooperation with the host country (Vietnam, Laos, or Cambodia) to search the suspected sites where the remains of American servicemen may be. Colonel Robert Gahagan served as the commander of one JTF-FA team for two years in Laos, and reported that all the teams are in a race against time. "Family members of our missing servicemen are aging," he said. "[Local] witnesses . . . are aging too. . . . And . . . in Laos, because of the soil conditions, human remains and physical evidence deteriorate very rapidly."

Even without a war, the search for remains is dangerous. On April 7, 2001, a helicopter carrying sixteen members of an MIA search team crashed into a mountainside due to heavy fog south of Hanoi. Seven Americans died in that crash—the first loss of life in the joint recovery program.

Above: Created in 1971 by the National League of Families of American Prisoners and Missing in Southeast Asia, this flag serves as a constant reminder of the plight of America's POWs/MIAs.

Opposite: A U.S. military honor guard accepting the coffins containing the remains of American MIAs found in North Vietnam in 1998.

QUICK FACTS

- The black granite of the Vietnam Veterans Memorial came from Bangalore, India. It was shipped to Vermont, where it was cut into panels. From there it went to Tennessee, where the names were cut into the panels. The cutting of the lettering was designed so that the sun would cast no shadows that might obscure or change the appearance of a name.

- In 2004 there were 58,235 names etched on the Vietnam Veterans Memorial. The Department of Defense, through the National Archives, has provided a database that has information about these people, as well as anyone else who served in Vietnam.

- According to the Department of Defense database, 40 percent of casualties among enlisted marines were teenagers. In the army 16 percent of its casualties were teenagers.

Above: A girl places a rose near the name of her grandfather, who was killed in the Vietnam War.

When the Vietnam War ended, a collective amnesia seemed to grip the American people. Not only did they want to forget the war, they wanted to have nothing to do with the men and women who fought in it. Vietnam veterans still in uniform wrestled with a military establishment traumatized by the experience. And Vietnam veterans who had been discharged discovered that they were now social outcasts. Sensational news reports about criminal acts committed by veterans suffering from post-traumatic stress syndrome even made getting a job difficult. James Hebron, a former marine, recalled, "This guy was telling me that he . . . wouldn't hire a Vietnam vet. . . . He thought we were all crazy."

A small group of people recognized that something was needed to help America and its veterans heal the still-raw emotional scars. In 1979 they organized the Vietnam Veterans Memorial Fund. On July 1, 1980 President Carter authorized the construction of a Vietnam veterans memorial on federal land in Washington, D.C., saying, "We are ready at last to acknowledge . . . the debt which we can never fully repay to those who served."

In a design competition held in the spring of 1981, architect Maya Ying Lin's polished, black V-shaped wall, containing the names of all who died in the war, was selected. "The Wall," as it came to be known, was not received with unanimous acclaim. While some people loved the design, others thought that it did not properly honor those who had fallen. As a result of insistent protests, a more traditional sculpture by Frederick Hart showing three soldiers was added. On November 11, 1993, to commemorate the contribution of servicewomen who participated in the war, the Vietnam Women's Memorial was placed near the Wall. Sculpted by Glenna Goodacre, it is of three nurses aiding a wounded soldier.

The location of these three memorials in the Washington Mall in Washington, D.C., has become a pilgrimage site for thousands. The Wall's initial controversy has since passed into acceptance. People search for the names of fallen loved ones, and as they do, they see their faces reflected in the polished, black granite surface. Some do pencil rubbings of the etched names on pieces of paper. Many leave flowers, letters, and mementos. Each day the National Park Service collects all the material left at the Wall and takes it away to be catalogued.

Opposite: The reflection of the *Three Servicemen* statue by Frederick Hart at the Vietnam Veterans Memorial.

QUICK FACTS

- Modern, unified Vietnam is officially named the Socialist Republic of Vietnam. The Communist Party of Vietnam rules the country through the National Assembly. The top three government officials are the general secretary, the president, and the prime minister.

- The Communists seized more than $1 billion worth of U.S. military equipment that had been left behind for the South Vietnamese Armed Forces. Some of the equipment was turned into scrap metal and other equipment, particularly the weapons, was sold to other nations.

- In 2003 the USS *Vandegrift* docked in the port of Ho Chi Minh City, the first U.S. Navy ship to dock in Vietnam since the end of the war. Many of the crew were sons and daughters of Vietnam War veterans.

- Nguyen Cao Ky was the prime minister of South Vietnam. He escaped the country when the Communists took over and started a new life as a businessman in California. He returned to visit his home country in 2004. During the visit, he said he believed it was time for reconciliation between the United States and Vietnam. "Younger men, in their fifties and sixties, are in charge in Hanoi," he said. "They know they have to get on with America."

1n 1975 Ho Chi Minh's dream of an independent and united Vietnam was achieved. The Communist government immediately embarked on a wide-range program of integration of the south. All private businesses and ownership of land were abolished. Farms were reorganized into collectives, which received all planting and harvesting orders from the government. Former officers in the South Vietnamese military and government officials were rounded up and sent to special reeducation camps, where they received political indoctrination lessons. For most, the periods in the reeducation camps lasted years. For some, the indoctrination also included torture.

The transition from a war economy to a peace economy proved to be very difficult for the Vietnamese government. The military consumed a third of the nation's budget—in the 1980s, Vietnam had approximately 1.2 million people in uniform, giving it the fourth largest military organization in the world. A famine in 1985 devastated the country, and inflation was running at four hundred to six hundred percent.

Gradually the government began making some reforms. A few private businesses were allowed to form, and farmers were allowed to market some produce privately instead of through the collective. International companies were allowed to establish businesses in the country. There were some political changes as well. Vietnam's government liberalized its censorship of the press and of writers and artists and also allowed for a measure of dissent. Nevertheless it remains a one-party, Communist dictatorship to this day.

After the war, the United States and Vietnam did not have any diplomatic relationship. The United States had imposed an economic embargo on Vietnam and made it illegal for U.S. nationals to travel to the country. The first steps in changing this adversarial relationship occurred in 1987, when officials from both countries opened talks to resolve the fate of MIA U.S. servicemen. In 1991 U.S. Secretary of State James Baker announced that the U.S. government was ready to take steps toward normalizing relations with Vietnam. In 1991 the travel ban for U.S. citizens was lifted. In 1994 President Bill Clinton announced the lifting of the trade embargo, and in 1995 announced the normalization of relations with Vietnam, including the opening of embassies and the exchange of ambassadors, saying, "The time has come to move forward and bind up the wounds from the war."

Opposite: Members of a farming co-op at Da Ton village haul harvested rice in from the fields.

Airmobile—Troops and supplies transported by helicopter.

Ambassador—The highest-ranking diplomatic representative of one country who is sent to another country.

Ammunition—Projectiles that are fired from weapons such as pistols, rifles, or cannons. These include bullets, cannon shells, and rockets.

Artillery—Weapons, such as cannons and mortars, that discharge ammunition.

Assault—A military attack upon fortified enemy forces.

Base camp—A semipermanent field headquarters and center for a military unit's combat operations in the immediate area.

Battalion—In the military table of organization, a tactical unit commanded by a lieutenant colonel. Infantry battalions usually contain nine-hundred troops and artillery battalions contained about five-hundred personnel. During the Vietnam War, American battalions were usually much smaller than that.

Battery—In the military, a grouping of cannons or mortars.

Blockade—The isolation of a region by military forces in order to prevent anyone or anything from going in or out.

Booby trap—An explosive charge hidden in a harmless object, which explodes on contact.

Boonies—Slang term for the field; jungles or swampy areas far from the comforts of civilization.

Bunker—A defensive fortification that is a an artificial hill of dirt and stone, which hides and protects a cannon or machine gun and its crew.

Campaign—A series of major military operations designed to achieve a long-range goal.

Cavalry—Originally combat troops mounted on horses. In modern military units, cavalry units are one of two types: air cavalry, which uses helicopters, and armored cavalry, which uses tanks.

"Charlie"—Slang for Viet Cong guerillas, taken from the military phonetic alphabet V (Victor) C (Charlie).

Claymore—A portable antipersonnel mine composed a numerous steel ball bearings detonated by an electric charge.

Communism—A social system created by Karl Marx, characterized by a classless society and the absence of ownership of private property.

Company—In the military a combat unit commanded by a captain and consisting of two or more platoons. It varies widely in size according to its mission.

Corps—The largest administrative unit in the army or marine corps. It is usually composed of two or more divisions, responsible for the defense of a military region.

Corpsman—An enlisted soldier or sailor trained to provide medical assistance, usually on a battlefield.

Democracy—Government by the people exercised either directly or through elected representatives.

DMZ—**De**militarized **Z**one. The border between North and South Vietnam established in 1954 at the Geneva Convention in which no troop movements or military operations were to occur.

Dustoff—The nickname for a medical evacuation helicopter mission.

Election—The selection by vote for individuals who want to occupy a public office such as the presidency.

Firefight—Exchange of small arms fire between opposing combat units.

Flank—The right or left side of a military unit.

Fortification—Defenses, usually walls and trenches, constructed to add strength to a military unit's position.

Friendly fire—The mistaken shooting of combat forces by allies or their own units.

Grunt—Slang for an infantryman in Vietnam; supposedly derived from the sound one made from lifting up his rucksack.

Guerilla—Soldiers of a resistance movement who are organized on a military or paramilitary basis.

Guerilla warfare—Military operations conducted in enemy-held or hostile territory by irregular, nonuniformed, predominantly indigenous forces.

Gunship—A helicopter armed with machine guns and rocket launchers.

Huey—Nickname for the UH-series helicopters; utility helicopter.

Hump—To march on patrol in enemy territory.

Infantry—Troops trained and equipped to fight on foot.

Insignia—A badge of office, rank, or membership in a group.

Medal of Honor—The highest military decoration awarded in all branches of the United States for gallantry and bravery above and beyond the call of duty in action against the enemy.

Medivac—Medical evacuation by helicopter; also called a dustoff.

MIA—**M**issing **i**n **A**ction, the official designation of military personnel whose location or fate is unknown, generally as a result of combat operations.

Mine—An explosive device usually planted beneath the ground, used to destroy enemy personnel or vehicles.

Napalm—Gasoline thickened to a gel and used as an incendiary weapon against enemy troops and positions.

Neutral—Belonging to neither side nor party.

Offensive—In military operations, a plan of attack.

Oppress—To keep down by the cruel or unjust use of power or authority.

Perimeter—In the military, the outer limits of a prepared base camp or other military position.

Platoon—In the military table of organization, a unit composed of approximately forty-five personnel, commanded by a lieutenant.

POW—**P**risoner **of W**ar. The official classification of military combatants captured by the enemy and housed in special fenced and guarded detention compounds called POW camps.

Reconnaissance—In military terms, the process of obtaining information about enemy intentions, troop movements, etc.

Rout—In military terms, the disorderly and panic-stricken retreat of defeated troops.

Search and destroy—Offensive operations designed to find and eliminate enemy forces.

Sentry—An armed guard of a military camp whose duty is to give a warning of danger.

Shrapnel—Fragments of the casing around an explosive device such as a bomb, a grenade, or a mine, resulting from the detonation of the device.

Siege—The surrounding and blockading of a town or military camp by an an opposing army that wants to capture it.

Sortie—In the military, the mission of one aircraft.

Soviet Union—From 1917 to 1991, the nation known officially as the Union of Soviet Socialist Republics; a nation composed of fifteen Communist-governed republics and dominated by its largest republic, Russia.

Squad—The smallest unit in the army and marine corps, usually composed of nine troops and commanded by a sergeant.

Tet—Vietnamese Lunar New Year.

Treaty—A formal agreement between two or more nations that contains terms of trade, military alliance, or other points of mutual interest.

Viet Cong—Communist guerilla forces stationed and conducting combat and terrorist operations in South Vietnam. Also known by the slang term "Charlie."

Viet Minh—Short for "Viet Nam Doc Lap Dong Minh Hoi," or the Vietnamese Independence League, the original political organization for Vietnamese patriots.

Vietnamization—U.S. policy initiated by President Nixon late in the war to turn over the fighting to the South Vietnamese army during the phased withdrawal of American troops.

BIBLIOGRAPHY

Anonymous. "Eating Out in Vietnam." *The Economist* Vol. 365, no. 8304 (December 19). London: 2002.

Appy, Christian G. *Patriots: The Vietnam War Remembered from All Sides.* New York: Viking, 2003.

Bergerud, Eric M. *Red Thunder, Tropic Lightning: The World of a Combat Division in Vietnam.* Boulder: Westview Press, 1993.

Bigler, Philip. *Hostile Fire: The Life and Death of First Lieutenant Sharon Lane.* Tampa, FL: Vandamere Press, 1996.

Burnam, Master Sgt. John C. USA (ret.). *A Soldier's Best Friend.* New York: Carroll & Graf Publishers, 2003.

Caputo, Philip. *A Rumor of War.* New York: Henry Holt and Company, 1996.

Carroll, Andrew, ed. *War Letters: Extraordinary Correspondence from American Wars.* New York: Scribner, 2001.

Chambers, John Whiteclay II. *The Oxford Companion to American Military History.* New York: Oxford University Press, 1999.

Cutler, Thomas J. *Brown Water, Black Berets: Coastal and Riverine Warfare in Vietnam.* Annapolis, MD: Naval Institute Press, 1988.

Daugherty, Leo. J. and Gregory Louis Mattson. *Nam: A Photographic History.* New York: MetroBooks, 2001.

Denenberg, Barry. *Voices from Vietnam.* New York: Scholastic, 1995.

Dupuy, Trevor N., Curt Johnson, and David L. Bongard. *The Harper Encyclopedia of Military Biography.* New York: HarperCollins, 1992.

Edelman, Bernard, ed. *Dear America: Letters Home from Vietnam.* New York: Norton, 1985.

Esper, George and the Associated Press. *The Eyewitness History of the Vietnam War, 1961–1975.* New York: Ballantine Books, 1983.

Estep, James. *Company Commander Vietnam.* Novato, CA: Presidio Press, 1991.

Furgurson, Ernest B. *Westmoreland: The Inevitable General.* Boston, MA: Little, Brown, 1968.

Halberstam, David. *The Best and the Brightest.* New York: Random House, 1992.

Hammel, Eric. *Khe Sanh: Siege in the Clouds: An Oral History.* Pacifica, CA: Pacifica Press, 1989.

Hayslip, Le Ly with Jay Wurts. *When Heaven and Earth Changed Places: A Vietnamese Woman's Journey from War to Peace.* New York: Plume, 1989.

Kelly, Orr. *Never Fight Fair!: Navy SEALs' Stories of Combat and Adventure.* Novato, CA: Presidio Press, 1995.

Lanning, Michael Lee and Ray William Stubbe. *Inside Force Recon: Recon Marines in Vietnam.* New York: Ballantine Books, 1989.

Lee, Lt. Col. Alex, USMC (ret.). *Force Recon Command: A Special Marine Unit in Vietnam, 1969–1970.* Annapolis, MD: Naval Institute Press, 1995.

Mangold, Tom and John Penycate. *The Tunnels of Cu Chi.* New York: Random House, 1985.

Mason, Robert. *Chickenhawk.* New York: Penguin Books, 1984.

McDonough, James R. *Platoon Leader.* Novato, CA: Presidio Press, 1985.

Mee, Charles L. Jr. *The End of Order: Versailles, 1919*. New York: Dutton, 1980.

Moore, Lt. Gen. Harold G., USA (ret.) and Joseph L. Galloway. *We Were Soldiers Once . . . and Young: Ia Drang, the Battle that Changed the War in Vietnam*. New York: HarperPerennial, 1993.

Prados, John. *Operation Vulture*. New York: Ibooks, 2002.

Prochnau, William W. *Once Upon a Distant War*. New York: Time Books, 1995.

Schwarzkopf, Gen. H. Norman and Peter Petre. *It Doesn't Take a Hero: General H. Norman Schwarzkopf, a Biography*. New York: Bantam Books, 1992.

Sheehan, Neil. *A Bright Shining Lie: John Paul Vann and America in Vietnam*. New York: Vintage Books, 1989.

Singlaub, Maj. Gen. John K., USA (ret.) with Malcolm McConnell. *Hazardous Duty: An American Soldier in the Twentieth Century*. New York: Summit Books, 1991.

Steinman, Ron. *The Soldiers' Story: Vietnam in Their Own Words*. New York: TV Books, 2000.

Sobel, Brian M. *The Fighting Pattons*. Westport, CT: Praeger, 1997.

Summers, Col. Harry G. Jr., USA (ret.). *On Strategy: A Critical Analysis of the Vietnam War*. Novato, CA: Presidio Press, 1982.

———. *The Vietnam War Almanac*. New York: Ballantine Books, 1999.

Tang, Truong Nhu, David Chanoff, and Doan Van Toai. *A Viet Cong Memoir*. New York: Vintage Books, 1985.

Tucker, Spencer C., ed. *The Encyclopedia of the Vietnam War: A Political, Social, and Military History*. New York: Oxford University Press, 2000.

Turley, Col. G. H., USMCR (ret.). *The Easter Offensive: Vietnam, 1972*. Novato, CA: Presidio Press, 1985.

West, F. J. Jr. *The Village*. Madison, WI: University of Wisconsin Press, 1985.

Whitburn, Joel. *Joel Whitburn Presents Billboard Top Ten Singles Charts, 1955–2000*. Menomonee Falls, WI: Record Research, 2001.

Woodruff, Mark W. *Unheralded Victory: The Defeat of the Viet Cong and the North Vietnamese Army, 1961–1973*. Tampa, FL: Vandamere Press, 1999.

Young, Marilyn B. *The Vietnam Wars 1945–1990*. New York: HarperCollins, 1991.

Zimmerman, Dwight Jon. "From Raiders to Recon." *Special Operations 2003*. Tampa, FL: Faircount, 2003.

Type the keywords *Vietnam War* into your search engine, and the result will produce more than five million sites devoted to the subject. They range from veterans' personal accounts, to unit histories, to educational forums, to Web site companions to documentaries and official government sites. Below are just a few of the useful sites:

AMERICAN EXPERIENCE: VIETNAM ONLINE

www.pbs.org/wgbh/amex/vietnam

The Web site companion for the public television documentary. Contains graphics, photographs, extensive text, and related links.

BATTLEFIELD: VIETNAM

www.pbs.org/battlefieldvietnam

A Web site companion to the PBS documentary on the Vietnam War. An extensive site on the subject, complete with photographs, charts and maps, and links to other sites.

POW/MIA HOME PAGE

lcweb2.loc.gov/pow/powhome.html

The Library of Congress Web site containing information and updates on the Vietnam War–era prisoner-of-war/missing-in-action database.

STATISTICS ABOUT THE VIETNAM WAR

www.vhfcn.org/stat.html

An in-depth compilation of facts and statistics about the Vietnam War.

VIETNAM: A COUNTRY STUDY

lcweb2.loc.gov/frd/cs/vntoc.html

The Library of Congress Web site that contains an in-depth history and country profile of Vietnam.

VIETNAM EMBASSY HOMEPAGE

www.vietnamembassy-usa.org

The official Web site of the embassy of the Socialist Republic of Vietnam in the United States of America. Contains the latest information and photographs about Vietnam, its people, culture, and economy. It also contains historical information about the country and the Vietnam War.

VIETNAM VETERANS HOMEPAGE

www.vietvet.org

An interactive online forum for Vietnam veterans, their families, friends, and anyone interested in the Vietnam War.

VIETNAM VETERANS MEMORIAL

www.nps.gov/vive

The National Parks Service interactive Web site for the Vietnam Veterans Memorial.

128

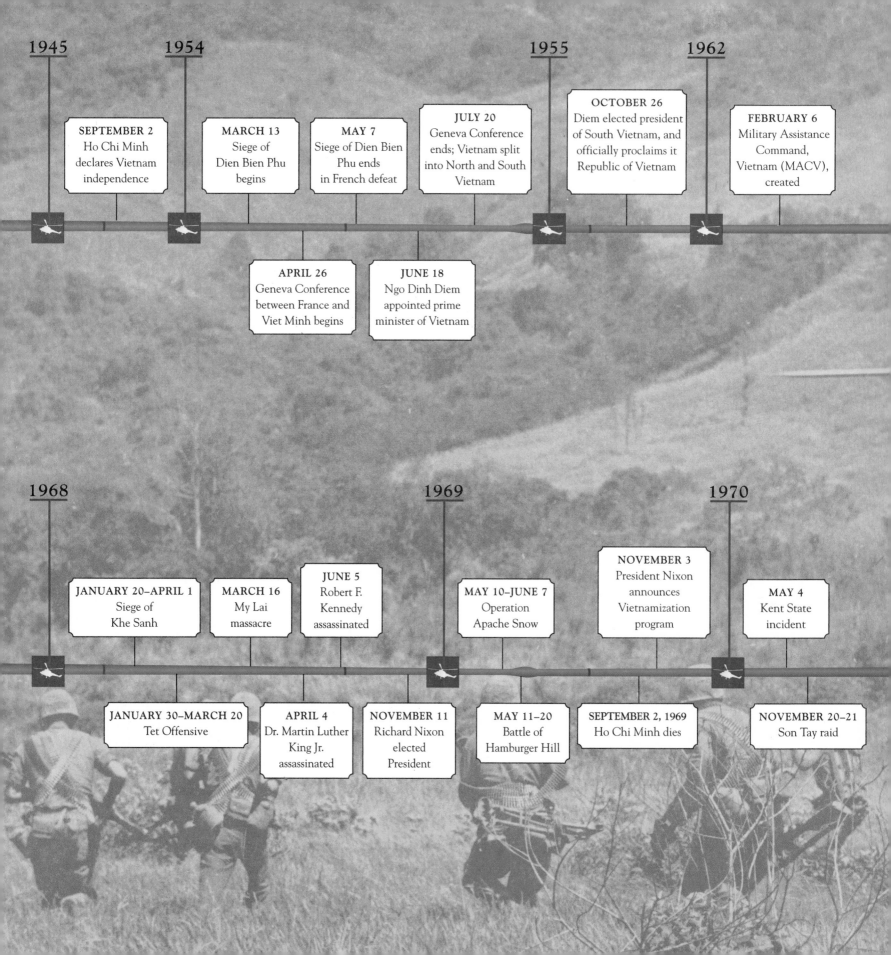

1945

SEPTEMBER 2
Ho Chi Minh
declares Vietnam
independence

1954

MARCH 13
Siege of
Dien Bien Phu
begins

MAY 7
Siege of Dien Bien
Phu ends
in French defeat

JULY 20
Geneva Conference
ends; Vietnam split
into North and South
Vietnam

1955

OCTOBER 26
Diem elected president
of South Vietnam, and
officially proclaims it
Republic of Vietnam

1962

FEBRUARY 6
Military Assistance
Command,
Vietnam (MACV),
created

APRIL 26
Geneva Conference
between France and
Viet Minh begins

JUNE 18
Ngo Dinh Diem
appointed prime
minister of Vietnam

1968

JANUARY 20–APRIL 1
Siege of
Khe Sanh

MARCH 16
My Lai
massacre

JUNE 5
Robert F.
Kennedy
assassinated

1969

MAY 10–JUNE 7
Operation
Apache Snow

NOVEMBER 3
President Nixon
announces
Vietnamization
program

1970

MAY 4
Kent State
incident

JANUARY 30–MARCH 20
Tet Offensive

APRIL 4
Dr. Martin Luther
King Jr.
assassinated

NOVEMBER 11
Richard Nixon
elected
President

MAY 11–20
Battle of
Hamburger Hill

SEPTEMBER 2, 1969
Ho Chi Minh dies

NOVEMBER 20–21
Son Tay raid